It is Written

Daily Truth to Face the Lies We Battle

Courtney Hope Wilson

To my mother, June Wilson. Thank you for always supporting my dreams and raising me to know God. Thank you for always praying for me and never giving up on me. I love you.

Contents

Introduction

God's word is a powerful tool. It's a weapon for good and a sword of defense. It's fully alive and breathing in the present. This is why even Jesus, the son of God Himself, used scripture to fight the lies of Satan. While Jesus was fasting in the wilderness for 40 days and nights, the devil tried to tempt Him. Jesus knew exactly which scriptures to use to speak truth over the lies of Satan. He would make a powerful statement in replying to Satan with *"It is written"* followed by quoting God's truth. This is such a powerful moment because even Jesus faced temptation, but He shows us how to overcome. His example shows us what we need to fight with when attacked with the lies of the enemy.

In Matthew 4:1-11, we see this story of Jesus unfold:

"Then Jesus was led by the Spirit into the wilderness to be tempted by the devil. After fasting forty days and forty nights, he was hungry. The tempter came to him and said, "If you are the Son of God, tell these stones to become bread." Jesus answered, "It is written: 'Man shall not live on bread alone, but on every word that comes from the mouth of God.'" Then the devil took him to the holy city and had him stand on the highest point of the temple. "If you

are the Son of God," he said, "throw yourself down. For it is written: "'He will command his angels concerning you, and they will lift you up in their hands, so that you will not strike your foot against a stone.'" Jesus answered him, "It is also written: 'Do not put the Lord your God to the test.'" Again, the devil took him to a very high mountain and showed him all the kingdoms of the world and their splendor. "All this I will give you," he said, "if you will bow down and worship me." Jesus said to him, "Away from me, Satan! For it is written: 'Worship the Lord your God, and serve him only.'" Then the devil left him, and angels came and attended him."

The enemy is cunning and even knows scripture himself, but as it says in John 8:44, *"…he was a murderer from the beginning, not holding to the truth, for there is no truth in him. When he lies, he speaks his native language, for he is a liar and the father of lies."* Satan doesn't speak truth and he twists everything around to deceive us. God's Word is powerful. The more we have it in our hearts, the more equipped we will be to fight off the lies of the enemy.

Our fight is deeper than what we see on the surface. In 2 Corinthians 10:3-5 it says, *"For though we live in the world, we do not wage war as the world does. The weapons we fight with are not the weapons of the world. On the contrary, they have divine power to demolish strongholds. We demolish arguments and every pretension that sets itself up against the knowledge of God, and we take captive every thought to make it obedient to Christ."*

Our thought life and the words we allow to take hold in our hearts have a huge impact on our lives. By making our thoughts obedient to Christ, we are weighing them against God's truth. God shows us throughout scripture who we are and the identity we have in Him. When a thought enters our minds if it doesn't align with what God says about us we should throw it out.

Unfortunately, we have all faced words that have caused us to believe lies about ourselves. It's time to take back what the enemy stole from us and fight with God's truth. In Hebrews 4:12 it tells us, *"For the word of God is alive and active. Sharper than any double-edged sword, it penetrates even to dividing soul and spirit, joints and marrow; it judges the thoughts and attitudes of the heart."* This scripture is a great visual for how to use God's word to fight the lies we face. It's time to recognize those lies and begin to remove the lie with the Truth.

This book is designed to be a quick reference tool that pulls scripture together as it relates to common life experiences and feelings we face. My hope is that you will be able to read the scriptures in each section when you are facing those feelings and understand God's truth. Through understanding God's truth, you can begin to overcome the lies of the enemy. I encourage you to find and highlight these scriptures in your Bible as well and speak them over yourself. Whether you are feeling depressed, anxious, overwhelmed or one of the other feelings highlighted in the chapters, use the scriptures to speak truth over the lies.

I pray that you will take God's truth to heart and begin to understand your full identity in Him. Pray His scripture during your prayer time and pray against the lies of the enemy. It's important to call out and recognize any lie that you've believed by bringing it into the light. Find a trusted mentor or friend who serves as godly counsel in your life and begin to work through the lies and have them pray the truth over you. I hope this book is just the beginning of declaring truth over the lies you face and that you will begin to seek God's word every day to overcome the lies of the enemy.

You are a child of God

Salvation Prayer

If you are reading this book and don't yet have a relationship with Jesus, I want to introduce you to Him. We were created by a loving Father who has a plan and purpose for our lives. Until we know Him, our lives tend to feel empty. Satan tries to distract us from finding Jesus by leading us to fill the void with everything else. Friend, I'm here to tell you today that you can find fullness in Jesus. If this sounds good to you and you want to begin that relationship right now, pray this where you are:

Dear Jesus, thank you for meeting me where I am. I recognize that I need You in my life and that my life is empty without You. I believe in You and I believe You are the Son of God and that You died for my sins. I ask that You would come into my heart and be my Savior. Please forgive me for any sin in my life. I turn from my past and ask that You would help me to do Your Will. I surrender today and give You control of my life. Thank you for saving me. In Jesus name, Amen.

Friend, I'm so glad you made this decision today! I would encourage you to find a local church to get involved in and find godly community. I hope this book will continue to bless you and help you to overcome any lie in your life.

You belong here

one

Identity, Calling, Belonging, Purpose

This chapter is all about understanding your identity in Christ. The enemy wants more than anything to distract you from your purpose and lie to you about your identity. These can be some of the deepest lies we face because many of them stem from the moment we were born. God wants you to understand your true identity in Him.

He has an incredible plan for your life and He made you uniquely to accomplish that plan. When we understand our identity in Christ, we will never feel more fulfilled. Many of us search our whole lives to fill a hole in our heart that can only be filled by Jesus. This is because we are all made in Christ's image and only He can fill in the gaps about our identity.

Scripture

"For I know the plans I have for you," declares the Lord, "plans to prosper you and not to harm you, plans to give you a hope and a future."

-Jeremiah 29:11

Devotional

If you're feeling a little lost in your purpose today and unsure of your calling, remember this verse. God created you with a distinct purpose. He has plans for you and they are good! When the Lord was speaking this, the Israelites were in captivity. They were in the midst of a valley season where the storm of life seemed endless. God wanted to remind them of their purpose and He wants to remind you as well.

We don't have to know our future or even our exact calling, we just have to know that we have one. We have to remember when the season of waiting is long and the enemy tries to confuse us in our purpose, God's plan is bigger. We will walk through difficult seasons and seasons of growth, but at the end of the day God's plan for us is good and full of hope. He chose for you to be here and we have to embrace that in our identity.

Prayer

Father, thank you for reminding me of my purpose today. I pray that You will continue to help me see my purpose in every season. Help me to hold fast to my identity in You. I pray against any lies from the enemy about my identity and calling. I pray that You will continue to grow me and reveal my calling to me. I want what you want Lord and I surrender my own will to Your good and perfect will. In Jesus name, Amen.

Thoughts

Scripture

"For we are God's handiwork, created in Christ Jesus to do good works, which God prepared in advance for us to do."
-Ephesians 2:10

Devotional

Friend, how amazing is it that we are all God's handiwork! We were created to do good works which were prepared in advance. That means before we ever thought about our purpose or identity, God already had it planned. He orchestrated for us to be here with purpose already in us. He thought of you and decided the world needed you. He thought of you and decided to create you so that the two of you could partner in your purpose to make a difference for His kingdom.

When the enemy begins to make us question why we are here or why we were born, we can state this truth. We were created on purpose with purpose. The enemy wants nothing more than to stop us from fulfilling God's purpose for our lives. He knows if we live out our purpose, then we will win people for Christ. So, don't believe the lies that cause you to doubt your calling or your identity in Christ. God made you uniquely and wants you to use your unique passions to make a difference for Him.

Prayer

Father, thank you for creating me on purpose. Thank you for the good works You have planned for me. Help me to keep my eyes on You and on my purpose when the world gets me down. Help me to stay eternally focused when things on earth seem hard. I pray that You would help me to embrace and know my identity in Christ and that You would guide me in my calling. I want to use my gifts and talents to glorify You, Lord. In Jesus name, Amen.

Thoughts

Scripture

"But you are a chosen people, a royal priesthood, a holy nation, God's special possession, that you may declare the praises of him who called you out of darkness into his wonderful light."

-1 Peter 2:9

Devotional

This truth is so incredible! God calls us out of darkness into His wonderful light. He chose for us to be here and we are His special possession. Take a second to breathe that in today. You are chosen and called. Don't let anyone ever make you feel otherwise. Don't believe any lie that tells you that you aren't meant to be here or that you were a mistake. God's truth tells us we are chosen, which means we were destined to be here in this very moment. He planned for you to be here no matter how you were brought into this world. The enemy tries to keep us in darkness about our identity, but God calls us out of that darkness into His light.

We are reminded of God's light when we take time to praise Him. If you're feeling confused about your purpose or identity then speak this truth over yourself today and turn on some worship music. Find things that you are thankful for and begin to thank God for that today. We are children of the Kingdom of God, which means you are royalty. Your identity is in the God most high and no one can take that from you. Stand firm in who you are in Christ and throw out the lies from the enemy!

Prayer

Father, thank you for choosing me to be here. It's a privilege to serve your kingdom. I pray against any lies from the enemy that causes me to doubt my identity in You. I declare Your truth over my life that I am chosen, royal and holy. I ask that You would remove any darkness in my life and help me to walk confidently in Your light. I praise You today and thank you for all You do in my life and all You created me to be. I ask for Your will and direction in my life as I continue to follow You. In Jesus name, Amen.

Thoughts

Scripture

"Before I formed you in the womb I knew you, before you were born I set you apart; I appointed you as a prophet to the nations."

-Jeremiah 1:5

Devotional

You belong here! You are set apart! Never believe the lie that tells you anything different. God knew you would exist before you were conceived or thought of by your parents. He formed you and chose for you to be here. Before you were even born, He designed your purpose and set you apart. Being set apart means that God waited until the perfect moment for you to be born and created you with a unique purpose. God also appoints us to be a witness for His Kingdom. Being a prophet to the nations doesn't necessarily mean you have to have the gift of prophesy. It means you are here to speak life over your sphere of influence (your nation) and shine the light of God where you go.

Hold onto this truth today and walk confidently in the purpose God's given you. Stand firm in your identity and know that you belong here. Cast out any thoughts that contradict this truth. Continually seek God to better understand who He created you to be. Be content where He has you because His divine purpose is always on time and His plan is perfect. Take heart knowing that the God of the universe is paying attention to you and He wants the best for your life. God also wants you to use your life to glorify Him to advance the Kingdom of Heaven. We find true fulfillment when we operate out of our identity in Christ and live out His purpose for our lives.

Prayer

Father, thank you for knowing me and setting me apart. Thank you for appointing me to be here as a witness for You. I come against any lie of the enemy that causes me to question my identity and I declare Your truth over my life that I am set apart and that I belong here. I pray that You would show me Your will in my current season. I ask You to speak to me and show me how I can use my gifts and talents for Your Kingdom. In Jesus name, amen.

Thoughts

Scripture

"No, in all these things we are more than conquerors through him who loved us. For I am convinced that neither death nor life, neither angels nor demons, neither the present nor the future, nor any powers, neither height nor depth, nor anything else in all creation, will be able to separate us from the love of God that is in Christ Jesus our Lord."

-Romans 8:37-39

Devotional

You are made to be more than a conqueror! No matter what we face in life or what comes our way we can conquer through Christ's love. How amazing is it that we don't have to earn His love? We already have it! Nothing can even separate us from God's love! What an incredible promise! This verse is such a powerful reminder of God's love and purpose in our lives. Whatever lie you've been told about your past, lay it at the cross and remember this truth today.

No matter what you've done or how far you've strayed, God still has a purpose for you. No matter how many pages we've added to the story of our lives, He still has the ending already written. We just have to embrace His love and surrender to Him. We have to choose to lay it all down and follow His plan for us. We can be conquerors through Jesus. We can overcome and change lives with His love. Your identity is founded in the love of Christ and when we embrace that we can live from His love instead of for His love. When we do that we no longer live for others love, but to love them.

Prayer

Father, thank you for Your incredible love! I'm so blown away that it can never be separated from me. I'm so thankful that I don't have to earn Your love but that You already love me. Help me to operate in my God-given identity and from a place of love. Help me to be fulfilled by You and Your love instead of seeking it through people. I ask that You would help me to overcome the lies and be a conqueror. I pray that others would experience Your love through my life. In Jesus name, amen.

Thoughts

Scripture

"For he chose us in him before the creation of the world to be holy and blameless in his sight. In love he predestined us for adoption to sonship through Jesus Christ in accordance with his pleasure and will."

-Ephesians 1:4-5

Devotional

When the world gets loud and you're feeling lost or unseen, remember this truth. God sees you and He chose you. Through His love He destined for you to be His child and made a way for this through Jesus. God wants good things for your life and wants you to understand your identity is in Him. Our identity is not in the world or in social media. Our identity is not in our significant other or lack thereof. Our identity is not in what we do. Our identity is solely in Christ. We find our identity when we surrender to God and give our hearts to Jesus. When we choose to invite Christ into our lives, we begin to live freely and fully.

After that we begin to understand our identity and calling. While each of us have different callings and purposes, our ultimate calling is to be holy and blameless and to love God and love others well. We will all do this in the unique way God created us, but it all has the same end goal. Rest in this today that you have a purpose and your identity is in Christ. Don't let the enemy deceive you or tell you lies about who you are or are not. Hold onto who God says you are and speak this truth over yourself.

Prayer

Father, thank you for choosing me and adopting me. Help me to daily find my identity in You and in Your love. I ask that You would guide me in my calling and purpose to use my gifts for You. I pray that You would help me to hold onto Your truth and that You would protect me from any lie of the enemy. I just want to do Your will and I surrender to You daily. Thank you for how You love me. In Jesus name, Amen.

Thoughts

Scripture

"Those who live according to the flesh have their minds set on what the flesh desires; but those who live in accordance with the Spirit have their minds set on what the Spirit desires."

-Romans 8:5

Devotional

Strive today to let the Spirit take the lead in your life. When we are followers of Christ, we have the Holy Spirit in us, guiding us. Our identity is made in Christ's image which means we are made of three parts just as He is. We are made up of spirit, soul and body. Often times things can get out of order in our lives. When we allow the flesh to lead, we are driven by the desires of our flesh which can cause us to easily sin. When we allow the soul to lead, we are driven by our emotions, which can cause us to feel chaotic. However, when we allow the Spirit to lead, we will live out of our Godly desires. We will live out of the fruits of the Spirit.

This is an important part of understanding our identity. The world often tells us we have to live by flesh or soul, but God's word tells us to live according to the Spirit. We need all three parts, but they have to be in the right order to lead us well. This is why we fast as Christians to reset the order. When we fast we "starve" the other two while feeding the Spirit. What you feed the most is what will lead you. We have to be disciplined enough not to let the flesh or soul have the driver's seat in our lives, but to allow them to ride along with the Spirit driving. This doesn't mean we have to constantly fast, it just means we have to develop a discipline to feed our Spirit and to know God's truth.

Prayer

Father, thank you for opening my eyes to learn more about my identity. I pray that You would reset the order of my identity and help my Spirit to lead me. Help me not give in to the desires of the flesh or soul. I speak against the lies of the enemy right now and declare this truth over my life that the Spirit will lead me. I thank you for Your grace and guidance. In Jesus name, Amen.

Thoughts

You are forgiven

Two

Unforgiveness, Anger, Bitterness, Offense

This chapter is for those moments when you find it hard to forgive. It's for those moments you find yourself angry, bitter or taking offensive to something in your life. These moments can be the hardest to deal with because of the emotion that surrounds them.

The truth found in the scriptures in this chapter shed light on how we can learn to forgive and overcome the lie of the enemy. Our life can be full of freedom when we learn how to forgive, let go and let God handle our problems. There's so much peace that can be found in God's truth and a huge weight can be lifted off of our lives when we give it all to Him.

Scripture

"But I tell you, love your enemies, and pray for those who persecute you."

-Matthew 5:44

Devotional

Forgiving your enemy may be the last thing you want to do when you're hurt. It's hard to pray for someone or a situation that left you hurting, but God's truth will set you free. When we pray for someone that hurt us, a healing begins to happen in our hearts. When we speak life over that person or situation, we begin to find our own freedom. This doesn't mean you need to allow that person back into your life. If you have faced impossible situations or abuse, it's not a safe situation to approach those people. If we can do what this verse says, then we can find true freedom in our spirit and souls.

When we find this freedom, we are no longer in bondage to unforgiveness, anger, bitterness or offense. We take away the enemy's power by declaring God's truth. Choosing to forgive someone is by no means saying what they did was okay. It wasn't okay. Forgiveness is letting God handle it for you and taking it off of your shoulders. I once heard it said that harboring unforgiveness is like setting yourself on fire and hoping the other person will die from smoke inhalation. Unforgiveness is only hurting ourselves and God wants a better life for us. He forgave us of all our sins and in return He asks us to forgive others. God wants to carry this burden for you and set you free.

Prayer

Father, thank you for showing me how to forgive. While it's hard to think about the situation surrounding the unforgiveness in my life, I know that I need to give it to You. I know that You will handle this situation. Help me to forgive the person that hurt me. I pray for their wellbeing and that You will help them to realize their wrong doings. I ask You to heal me and help me to find freedom from this. Father, please remove any unforgiveness, bitterness, anger or offense from me and replace it with your love, peace and joy. In Jesus name, Amen.

Thoughts

Scripture

"Make every effort to live in peace with everyone and to be holy; without holiness no one will see the Lord. See to it that no one falls short of the grace of God and that no bitter root grows up to cause trouble and defile many."

-Hebrews 12:14-15

Devotional

We're called to live in peace with everyone. This can be hard to do at times. Just because we live in peace doesn't mean we are in relationship with those who have hurt us. Living in peace simply means that we are living in peace in our hearts and allowing God to handle the situation for us. When we harbor unforgiveness, anger, bitterness or offense it brings us dis-ease. It eats away at us and it makes it hard for us to find peace. It's not our role to hold onto the hurt, but to give it to God and find a way to forgive.

I don't know much about gardening, but I do understand that roots are significant. They grow deep and are hard to fully extract once they begin to grow. They spread out and take over underneath the surface. Once we begin to let a root take hold in our lives, we have to work really hard with God's help to find freedom from it and uproot it. What we sow into ourselves is what will overflow out of ourselves. If we have any roots of anger, bitterness, unforgiveness or offense in our hearts, we will begin to spill out anger, rage and bitterness onto others. This is why we need God's grace and freedom. We need Him to remove the pain, roots and hurt so we can live free and pour out His love.

Prayer

Father, thank you for this truth today. I ask if there is any unforgiveness, bitterness, anger or offense in my heart that You would please remove it. Please remove any roots of these in my life and cleanse me so that I can pour out love instead. I ask that You would heal my heart from the situation that hurt me and that You would take this burden for me. Thank you for Your forgiveness and Your freedom. Help me to have full freedom from this hurt. In Jesus Name, Amen.

Thoughts

Scripture

"Do not conform to the pattern of this world, but be transformed by the renewing of your mind. Then you will be able to test and approve what God's will is- his good, pleasing and perfect will."

-Romans 12:2

Devotional

We live in a fallen world that often misleads our ideas and thoughts. We live in a world where revenge and vengeance are just a click away. We see it all the time on the internet- the cruel comments, the embarrassing photos. It's hard to escape, but God's word calls us to rise above. We can't conform to the way the world does things. When we're hurt and feeling unforgiveness, anger, bitterness or offense we have to rise above how the world handles these things. We need to seek God to be renewed and restore our hearts. It's God's will for us to portray the fruits of the spirit and surrender daily to Him.

This is hard to do when we're experiencing these feelings, but we can cling to God's Word and pray through it using this verse. We can trust that God will take care of the situation whether on this side of heaven or the other side. We can focus on ourselves and our relationship with God instead of re-living the hurt. When we work on this and do this we will be able to focus more on God's will for our lives. We won't be distracted by the feelings, but will be focused on the eternal impact we can make on this earth.

Prayer

Father, thank you for this reminder and this truth today. Please renew my mind and set it on eternal things. Help me not to conform to the world but to conform to You. God, I let go of all the unforgiveness, anger, bitterness, and offense and give it to You to handle. Please heal my heart and hear my prayer. I just want to do Your will. I surrender all of this to You. In Jesus name, Amen.

Thoughts

Scripture

"My dear brothers and sisters, take note of this: everyone should be quick to listen, slow to speak and slow to become angry, because human anger does not produce the righteousness that God desires."

-James 1:19-20

Devotional

You may have heard the saying that there's a reason God gave us two ears and one mouth. It can be so easy to react in situations that hurt us. It can be hard not to say something back when someone else is mean. Remember this truth today and choose to respond with God's love. If we respond with self-righteousness and anger it only heats the situation more. It's not an easy thing to hold back our reactions when we find ourselves in these types of situations. We have to continually seek God and ask the Holy Spirit to lead us. When we live a Spirit led life, our flesh and soul are less likely to react in a harsh way.

God knows how harmful and vengeful human anger can be and that's why He doesn't desire it for our lives. Let's continue to seek Him in the hard situations and lean on Him. Life is going to continually throw us curve balls. When we let God deal with it we can find our own bit of peace. It's a choice to not take offense or be angry. It's okay if you feel these things. The key is to not let your feelings linger and become the driver in your life because it will only lead to misery. When we let God lead us and hold us it's so much more joyous.

Prayer

Father, I pray today that You would help me not to react but to respond with Your love. Help me to hold my tongue in tough situations. I ask for the Holy Spirit to guide me. I ask that You would remove any anger, bitterness, offense or unforgiveness in my life. Show me the areas where I'm still harboring these feelings. Help me to listen more and react less. I also ask for healing and freedom from my current situation that has hurt me. In Jesus name, Amen.

Thoughts

Scripture

"It is for freedom that Christ has set us free. Stand Firm, then, and do not let yourselves be burdened again by a yoke of slavery."

-Galatians 5:1

Devotional

Whatever it is you are feeling entrapped by today, just know God has freedom for you. We can stand firm and confident in His truth. We no longer have to be burdened by a yoke of slavery. A yoke is a farming tool that was placed around the neck of a pair of oxen to steer them through the fields. In this verse it's referring to the yoke of the law before Christ. Christ came to pay for our sins and take away our burdens. This means we no longer have to wear the yoke around our neck of unforgiveness, bitterness, offense or anger. We can ask God to heal and remove it from us. A related verse, Matthew 11:28-30, speaks to God carrying our burden for us. It talks about casting our worries on Him and taking His yoke upon us because His burden is light and His yoke is easy. How amazing is that? Our God is so caring that He willingly does this for us if we just ask Him.

I know how difficult it can be to let go of these feelings in particular. It seems like holding onto them is the only part we have control over in our situation. However, it's the very thing that's keeping us in bondage in our situation. The enemy will constantly try to keep us in slavery to our situation and feelings. But this truth tells us that we can let it go by giving it to God. We can have freedom through Christ!

Prayer

Father, thank you for this reminder today. Thank you that I can stand firm in Your truth when the lies try to convince me otherwise. I declare freedom over my situation and feelings today and ask You to remove my burden. I'm giving this to You Lord, every part of it. I fully surrender and ask You to search my heart for any hidden roots I need to remove. Help me to see Your truth and to stand on You when the world around me shakes. In Jesus name, Amen.

Thoughts

Scripture

"In your anger do not sin: do not let the sun go down while you are still angry, and do not give the devil a foothold... Get rid of all bitterness, rage, and anger, brawling and slander, along with every form of malice. Be kind and compassionate to one another, forgiving each other, just as Christ God forgave you."

-Ephesians 4:26-27;31-32

Devotional

It's easy when we experience pain in our hearts to react in a way that hurts someone back. We've all had our moments when we said something out of anger, offense or bitterness just to hurt the person that hurt us. God's truth today is calling us beyond that reaction. He wants us to be aware of the sin that comes with anger and to rid ourselves of it. We are only guaranteed today so be sure to reconcile in your heart your situation and find forgiveness even if the other person doesn't do the same thing. It may not be a feasible situation for you to reconcile with the other person, but you can still reconcile in your own heart.

If we don't reconcile and we continue on the path of hurt by harboring these feelings it will give the devil a foothold in our lives. It's like setting the alarm on your home, but leaving the window cracked open where the burglar can enter. We don't want to leave any room for the enemy to destroy our lives with his lies. Our Father in heaven forgave us and we have to find a way to forgive in our hearts. God's truth reminds us that no matter what we need to be kind, compassionate and forgive. While it's a hard thing to do, it will help us to live a free life and follow God's will.

Prayer

Father, I ask if there is any unforgiveness or hurt in my heart that You would reveal it to me and forgive me for it. What the other person did is not okay, but I don't want them to cause me not to have freedom through You. I ask that You would help me to overcome these thoughts and feelings. I ask You to help me reconcile in my own heart and that You would deal with them. I pray for healing today. In Jesus name, Amen.

Thoughts

Scripture

"Therefore, as God's chosen people, holy and dearly loved, clothe yourselves with compassion, kindness, humility, gentleness, and patience. Bear with each other and forgive one another if any of you has a grievance against someone. Forgive as the Lord forgave you. And over all these virtues put on love, which binds them all together in perfect unity."

-Colossians 3:12-14

Devotional

What an incredible reminder! We are chosen, holy and dearly loved! Let this truth sink into your heart and mind today. It can be hard to remember our true identity when we are living from a place of unforgiveness, anger, bitterness or offense. What we think and dwell on is what clothes us. If we dwell on the hurt then we will give an outward appearance of the feelings that go with the hurt. If we choose to give those feelings to God and forgive what hurt us we can begin to consciously clothe ourselves in good things. We can choose to wear compassion, kindness, humility, gentleness and patience. Others will notice this and see there's something different about us. Ultimately God's love is what allows all of these good feelings and virtues to clothe us.

God forgave us of all of our sins, no questions asked and in return He asks us to forgive others. God understands your situation and by forgiving them you aren't saying what happened is okay. He wants you to have freedom from it and allow Him to take care of it. When we forgive the other person, we have to truly mean it. We have to allow God to heal us and provide freedom in our lives. Our lives are so much better when we live cloaked in God's love!

Prayer

Father, thank you for allowing Your Son to die on the cross to forgive my sins. Help me to heal and have the courage to forgive those that have trespassed against me. Clothe me in compassion, kindness, humility, gentleness and patience. Help me to exude Your love to others. Thank you for the freedom only You can provide. In Jesus name, Amen.

Thoughts

You are accepted

three

Rejection, Abandonment, Loneliness

This chapter is for those dealing with feelings of rejection, abandonment and loneliness. Often times life can leave us feeling like we're outcasts or overlooked. We have experiences that cause us to feel like we're alone or rejected. This is hard because it hits directly to our core and identity. I understand the pain that is associated with these feelings and have felt it myself at times. It's something we have to work hard to overcome.

Unfortunately, we live in a fallen world where people often do things that leave us feeling hurt. The enemy loves to use that to isolate us and feed lies to us about our identity. The scriptures in this chapter remind us what God says about us. God loves you so incredibly much and He never leaves your side. Seek truth in His Word today and see what He says about you, His beloved.

Scripture

"For the sake of his great name the Lord will not reject his people, because the Lord was pleased to make you his own."

-1 Samuel 12:22

Devotional

Remember this truth today that God will never reject you. While we may experience rejection in this world and it may seem like no one is on our side, God loves you. He always accepts you and He will never reject you because He created you. He made you His own child and chooses you. Don't believe any lie that tells you otherwise. The enemy loves to hit us where it hurts most and he uses our past to taunt us. He loves to isolate us and feed us lies that we aren't wanted. Declare God's truth over the lies today!

Choose to see through God's eyes instead of the view of rejection. Often times when we've faced rejection, we begin to live life from that place instead of from a place of love. We automatically give in to the lie that we will always be rejected, but that's not what God wants for our lives. He wants us to live from a place of love because He first loved us. Nothing can separate us from that love and He will never reject or abandon you. In order to overcome the lies, we have to choose to believe God's truth.

Prayer

Father, thank you for reminding me of Your acceptance. Thank you for choosing me and loving me and never giving up on me. I ask that You would reveal to me any roots of rejection in my life and help me to overcome the lie so I can be free from rejection. I come against any lie of the enemy that tells me I'm rejected and I replace it with Your truth that I'm accepted and loved. Thank you for this truth. In Jesus name, Amen.

Thoughts

Scripture

"A father to the fatherless, a defender of widows, is God in his holy dwelling. God sets the lonely in families, he leads out the prisoners with singing; but the rebellious live in a sun-scorched land."

-Psalm 68:5-6

Devotional

If you're feeling lonely or abandoned today, take heart in this truth. God is a father to the fatherless. He defends you and He is a holy dwelling. He puts those who are lonely in families and sets us free with rejoicing. This verse is a beautiful truth of all that is possible through Christ. Never believe the lie that you are alone or that no one cares about you. God cares and He will provide you with community. He understands where you are and what you're going through today. We have to ask God for the right community. Then we have to take a step after praying by intentionally seeking out godly friendships. We have to be brave and ask those people to coffee or dinner so we can get to know them better. We will begin to see God's hand beautifully weaving relationships together in our lives.

Rest in the fact that no matter if you are close to your family or not, God will set you in a community that will feel like a family. If we show up, so will they. We have to be so careful not to isolate ourselves. The biggest way the enemy can lie to us is by isolating us and taunting us. If he can get us to believe the lies and step away from community, then he will trick us into feeling lonely and abandoned. Don't allow Satan to have that power over you. God has better for you and wants you to declare this truth by seeking Jesus and seeking community. He can heal you and restore you!

Prayer

Father, thank you for reminding me that I'm not alone or abandoned. I know that You are my Father and I know how much You love me. I pray against any lie that tells me I'm alone or abandoned today. I replace that lie with Your truth that You set me in a family and You are my Father and I can dwell in You. I declare that I'm no longer a prisoner to the lies but I can live fully and freely in Your love. I praise You today! In Jesus name, amen.

Thoughts

Scripture

"You are my hiding place; you will protect me from trouble and surround me with songs of deliverance."

-Psalm 32:7

Devotional

Whatever you are facing today, you can rest in God's presence. This verse reminds us that God is our hiding place, which essentially means He is our protection. This doesn't mean we won't ever face hardship or difficulties, but it means He will protect us. He will surround us with encouragement or songs of deliverance. God's truth will protect your thoughts when you continually declare His truth over the lies the enemy whispers to you. When you feel unseen, remember that God sees you. When you feel unknown, God knows you. We have to find our worth in God rather than the world. When we do this and hide in our Heavenly Father, we will know true freedom and fulfillment.

King David wrote this Psalm and he encouraged himself in the Lord. He faced many trials in life, including rejection. We can learn so much from how he interacted with God. Take a moment to encourage yourself in the Lord today through prayer and reading through the Psalms. It often helps to journal through our thoughts and write down what God says through scripture. As you encourage yourself by reading the Psalms, write down what the verses say about God's character and what He says about you. Run to God whenever you feel lonely, abandoned or rejected. Trust God to take care of you and heal you. Trust His truth to refuel you.

Prayer

Father, thank you for being my hiding place. Thank you for protecting me and surrounding me with encouragement. I pray that You would help me to heal from any lies of loneliness. I come against the lies of rejection and loneliness in the name of Jesus and declare Your love over my life. I know that my hope and identity is found in You not in others. I know that no matter what, You have a plan for my life and will protect me. I ask that You will daily encourage me and remind me that I'm never alone. In Jesus name, Amen.

Thoughts

Scripture

"So do not fear, for I am with you; do not be dismayed, for I am your God. I will strengthen you and help you; I will uphold you with my righteous right hand."

-Isaiah 41:10

Devotional

Friend you are not alone! God is always with you and He will never leave you. Rest in this truth today that God will strengthened and help you. He will uphold you. God loves you so incredibly much! He desires so much more for you and wants you to understand His truth. The enemy wants to trick you into believing that you are alone and abandoned. He does this by getting us when we are by ourselves and setting our focus on earthly desires instead of eternal desires. When Satan gets our focus off of God and onto our circumstances by showing us what we don't have, we begin to feel lonely and abandoned. God's truth defeats this lie!

God doesn't want us to fear because He is right there with us. He wants us to seek Him and rest in Him always especially when the lie gets loud. We have to declare this truth over our life. We have to trust that God truly is with us and allow Him to strengthen us by seeking Him. How incredible is it that our God cares so much about us that He never leaves us and He upholds us? That itself is encouraging because when we cling to that we can find so much freedom from our current circumstances.

Prayer

Father, thank you for reminding me that You are with me. I speak against loneliness and abandonment in the name of Jesus and replace it with Your strength and love. I pray that You will help me to overcome in my current situation and walk forward in the freedom You provide. I'm so thankful for all that I have in life. I'm thankful for everything You have provided for me. I'm thankful for ways that You will provide in the future. I pray that You will help my heart as I deal with this season. In Jesus name, Amen.

Thoughts

Scripture

"For you created my inmost being; you knit me together in my mother's womb. I praise you because I am fearfully and wonderfully made; your works are wonderful, I know that full well."

-Psalm 139:13-14

Devotional

You are here on purpose with purpose. Knitting is a tedious, careful practice and this verse shows us how carefully and purposefully God knit us into our mother's womb. We are not rejected because our existence has purpose no matter how we were born or where we are now. We are wonderfully made. If you read through this Psalm in its entirety, you'll see over and over God's love and purpose for you. We can see how intentional our Father was in choosing for us to be here.

No matter who has rejected you or caused you pain, declare God's truth over your life that you have purpose. You are loved and He decided the world needed someone like you. Rest in that truth and keep it handy any time you start to feel the lie of rejection creeping up. Your worth is not in other people or in what others say about you. Your worth is in what God says about you. Hold onto your identity in Christ and throw out the lies of the enemy!

Prayer

Father, thank you for Your love. Thank you for the purpose You have given me and continue to remind me that I belong to You. I come against the lies of rejection in the name of Jesus and replace the lies with Your truth that I am loved and fearfully and wonderfully made. I pray for healing from any roots of rejection and ask You to remove these roots in the name of Jesus. Thank you for Your healing power. In Jesus name, Amen.

Thoughts

Scripture

"But he said to me, "My grace is sufficient for you, for my power is made perfect in weakness." Therefore I will boast all the more gladly about my weaknesses, so that Christ's power may rest on me."

-2 Corinthians 12:9

Devotional

Whatever you may be feeling today, God's grace is enough for you. He covers you with His grace and loves you. If you feel like you've strayed too far or that you are abandoned, hold onto this truth today. God doesn't reject or abandon you, but gives grace in your weakness. He doesn't look at your past and reject you for it. He gives you grace and forgiveness. We can boast in our weakness because God's strength shines through it.

Don't believe the lies of the enemy when he whispers doubt after a rejection. Whether it was a job or a person that rejected you, take heart knowing that God has a plan for you. God will give you strength and will lead you to the exact place you need to be. Allow God's power to rest on you and learn to trust His plan. Lean on God in those moments of weakness when you feel lonely, rejected or abandoned. Seek his strength and power.

Prayer

Father, thank you for this truth today that Your grace is sufficient to cover me. Help me to lean on You when I feel rejected, abandoned or lonely. Cover me with Your strength. Help me to walk forward in Your strength and rest in Your power. I rebuke the lies of the enemy today and declare Your truth today that in my weakness Your power is made perfect and You have a plan for me. Heal my heart today. In Jesus name, Amen.

Thoughts

Scripture

"As he says in Hosea, "I will call them 'my people' who are not my people and I will call her 'my loved one' who is not my loved one.""

-Romans 9:25

Devotional

The truth in this verse is so powerful. If you feel rejected, abandoned or lonely, remember today that God sought you out to be His. God so desperately wants a relationship with you. Even when you stray away He wants you. This verse in Romans is referring to God calling the gentiles into His kingdom. This gives us hope because God is calling us His people and His loved one. Don't allow the enemy to tell you that you aren't loved or that you've gone too far to be in God's kingdom. This verse shows us God's truth. You are loved and you are God's people!

In this scripture, Paul speaking to the Gentiles and the Jews to help them understand their identity in Christ. This verse also references Hosea, which is a beautiful redemption story of God's love for us. God continually takes us back no matter how far we run or how much we reject Him. We can rest in these truth's today because we serve a loving Father whose unconditional love is always available. Declare today that you are a child of God and that He accepts you just as you are.

Prayer

Father, thank you for reminding me that I'm a child of God and that You call me beloved. Thank you for never giving up on me even when I've sometimes given up on You. I pray that You would heal any hurt in my heart from rejection, abandonment and loneliness. I come against any lie from the enemy that says I'm not loved or that I'm abandoned and I speak Your truth over those lies in Jesus name and declare that I am loved and I am Your child. I know today that I have Your unconditional love and that You accept me. Thank you, In Jesus name, amen.

Thoughts

You have purpose

four

Fear, Faithlessness, Doubt

This chapter is for when you are feeling faithless, fearful or doubtful. When our circumstances in life aren't turning out the way we imagined, we can begin to lose faith. We can begin to let fear set in our hearts while playing the "what if" game. We can begin to doubt everything.

This is a lie the enemy loves to tell us. He wants to get our focus on everything that is going wrong or could go wrong in our lives to instill fear. Satan wants to distract us from our purpose by causing us to doubt or lose faith. God desires for us to lean on Him and trust that He has a plan for us. Scripture proves God's love and promises to us over and over again. In those moments of doubt or fear, let's turn to God's truth to overcome the lies.

Scripture

"The Lord is my light and my salvation- whom shall I fear? The Lord is the stronghold of my life- of whom shall I be afraid?"

-Psalm 27:1

Devotional

If you feel fearful today, declare this truth. When God is on your side there's nothing to fear. Sometimes we will feel fear and we will have to do things afraid, but we can never let fear hold us back. This verse reassures us because it shows God is our light and Savior. He is also the stronghold of our lives. Stronghold in this verse means *a place that has been fortified so as to protect against attack*. How incredible is this when we are facing fear? God is like a fortress for us so we have no need to be afraid with Him on our side.

Face your fear today and speak this truth over the lies the enemy has told you. Satan has no power in your life so move forward in confidence that God is your stronghold! Sometimes we just have to do it afraid. It's okay if fear rides in the car with you, but don't let fear drive. Keep going and tell fear not today! Rest in God's strength and goodness. Hold onto His truth when fear comes knocking. You will be so glad you pushed through because on the other side of fear is so much more! God has more for your life and has so many plans for you.

If we let fear stop us then we will never accomplish all God has planned. This is the enemy's strategic plan to make you fearful enough that you won't move forward. However, we know God's truth and His protection to overcome this lie!

Prayer

Father, thank you for reminding me of this truth today. I ask that You would help me to overcome any fear in my life today. I pray against any lies of the enemy right now and declare Your truth that You are my stronghold, light and salvation. I pray that You will help me to move past the fear into my future. Help me to lean on Your strength and do Your will. In Jesus name, amen.

Thoughts

Scripture

"Peace I leave with you; my peace I give you. I do not give to you as the world gives. Do not let your hearts be troubled and do not be afraid."

-John 14:27

Devotional

If you are feeling fear or doubt today, rest in this truth. Jesus reminds us that He left us with peace. He reminds us that He gives us peace, but not like the world does. His peace is deeper. He doesn't want us to be troubled or afraid, but rather to live with peace. This is powerful because Jesus left us the holy spirit who provides this peace. The Holy Spirit lives inside of us as Christians, which means we already have peace inside of us. We just have to tap into that power of peace from the Holy Spirit.

The enemy will often instill fear in us through events in the world and make us afraid to do anything. However, as followers of Christ we are called above that fear. We have a secret weapon and that's the Holy Spirit. We can have a peace that surpasses all understanding. We can know at our core that God is in control and is moving in ways we can't yet see. When the world gets loud and your feeling fearful or doubting God's plan, hold onto His peace. Seek God in those moments and don't look at it through the world's lens. Declare God's truth to overcome the lies of the enemy. Jesus freely gives us peace and all we have to do is receive it.

Prayer

Father, thank you for Your peace today. I ask for You to give me peace today through the Holy Spirit and help me to overcome the fear in my life. I pray against any lie of the enemy today that is causing fear or doubt and I receive Your peace and strength in Jesus name. Help me to have a strong mind and to control my thoughts when fear tries to creep in. Help my heart not to be troubled today. In Jesus name, Amen.

Thoughts

Scripture

"He replied, "Because you have so little faith, Truly I tell you, if you have faith as small as a mustard seed, you can say to this mountain, "Move from here to there" and it will move. Nothing will be impossible for you.""

-Matthew 17:20

Devotional

How incredible is this truth? We all experience faithlessness at times. It can be hard to see something when it takes a while or doesn't happen how we thought it would. That's when the lies start to taunt us causing us to doubt our faith and God's faithfulness. This verse reminds us that it doesn't take a huge amount of faith to see movement. A mustard seed is a tiny little round seed about as big as a pin hole, yet it grows into a huge plant. Here God is showing us that if we have just a tiny bit of faith, we can tell a mountain to move. Wow!

Whatever lie is causing you to doubt or have faithlessness, tell it to move today in Jesus name. Declare God's truth over the lies and encourage your faith with this verse. Ask God for faith even if it's as small as a mustard seed. Ask God to remove the mountains standing in your way and walk forward in this truth today. Nothing is impossible with God! We just have to trust His goodness and have a little faith. He's moving on your behalf and hasn't forgotten you!

Prayer

Father, thank you for this truth today! I pray that You would help me to have faith and to remove any mountains in my life. I ask that You would continue to strengthen my faith. I come against any lies of the enemy right now causing faithlessness and declare Your truth that nothing is impossible with You. I trust You Lord and I know You have a plan and are moving in ways I can't even see. Thank you for being faithful always. In Jesus name, Amen.

Thoughts

Scripture

"Therefore I tell you, whatever you ask for in prayer, believe that you have received it, and it will be yours."

-Mark 11:24

Devotional

God hears your prayers. Every single one of them. Nothing is too small to pray about. God may not always answer in the way we think He will, but He is always good! If you are struggling with doubt today or have lost faith about what you've been praying for, remember this truth. We have to believe that we have received it in Jesus name and trust that God is going to do what is best. We have to be willing to submit to His will and trust His plans for our lives. We serve a big God and He wants us to pray big prayers!

God doesn't want us to lose hope in praying but to gain hope through our prayers. He will answer in the best timing possible and He is working on it even when we can't see it. God doesn't do anything half way and He knows exactly what we need. Don't let the enemy lie to you and cause you doubt. This truth reminds us that God answers prayers and He wants us to pray. If it's small enough to worry about then it's big enough to pray about! Remember this today and pray with courage. Receive the truth that God will answer!

Prayer

Father, thank you for this reminder today. I know that You are going to answer my prayers and when You do, it will be in the best way possible. You know what is best for me and You know what my future holds. I pray for faith and I receive what I've been praying for today. I come against any lie from the enemy that speaks fear, doubt or faithlessness to me. I replace the lie with Your truth that You will answer and are moving on my behalf. I know You are good and You love me deeply. In Jesus name, Amen.

Thoughts

Scripture

"But when you ask, you must believe and not doubt, because the one who doubts is like a wave of the sea, blown and tossed by the wind."

-James 1:6

Devotional

If you're facing doubt today, remember this truth. Doubt causes us to feel unstable and to easily fall. We have to declare God's truth today to overcome the lie of doubt. We have to stand firm in Christ by believing that God is good and has good plans for our lives. When we ask for something in prayer and it takes a while to receive, we can begin to doubt that God will come through for us. This verse reminds us that we must believe He will come through no matter what. Otherwise we will constantly feel uneasy when we focus on the doubt. We will feel tossed around just like waves in the ocean.

The ocean is a powerful thing. If we were to swim out in the deep ocean without a boat or anchor we would float away or drown. If we have an anchor holding us, we will be stable and safe. This is the same in our faith walk. If we begin to doubt, it's like letting go of the anchor. We begin to give into the lie that the enemy tells us and it pulls us further from the Truth. Cling to this truth today and believe what God says is true. He will come through for you and His timing is so perfect. When you start to doubt, put your focus back on God and remember His character.

Prayer

Father, thank you for this truth today. I believe that You are good and You will come through. I cast out any doubt or fear today that is causing faithlessness in my life. I proclaim Your truth and ask that You would help me not to doubt. I ask for courage to stay strong in my faith and that You would draw me closer to You. In Jesus name, Amen.

Thoughts

Scripture

"For the Spirit God gave us does not make us timid, but gives us power, love and self-discipline."

-2 Timothy 1:7

Devotional

If you're feeling fear, doubt or faithlessness today, declare this truth! Whatever lie the enemy has told you, remember that God has not given you a spirit of fear! God has given us the fruits of the Spirit so we must cling to that truth. We must cling to each fruit of the Spirit because it will help us to cast out the lies of the enemy. God gives us power, love and self-discipline. Part of that means we have to be self-disciplined to recognize and throw out the lies the enemy whispers. We can't give him any power!

God gives us the power through Jesus' name to cast out the enemy. He gives us love to power through the fear. He gives us self-discipline to overcome timidity. When we start to feel the fear and doubt creeping in we can speak this truth over ourselves. There's many times where I've been in a situation where I got scared or fearful and began to declare this truth in my heart to help me through the fear. The more I declared it, the less scared I became in the situation. We have to trust that God will protect us and we have to be brave in these moments.

Prayer

Father, thank you for this reminder today that You don't give us a spirit of fear. I declare this truth over my life right now. I come against the lies of the enemy that instill fear and doubt and I replace it with Your love and power. Help me to be self-disciplined to overcome my doubts and fears. Help me to hold fast to Your truth when I feel scared. I ask for Your constant protection. In Jesus name, Amen.

Thoughts

Scripture

"Say to those with fearful hearts, 'Be strong, do not fear; your God will come, he will come with vengeance; with divine retribution he will come to save you.'"

-Isaiah 35:4

Devotional

When you are facing fear or doubt, declare this truth over yourself. Tell yourself to be strong and not to fear. Trust that God is with you and will protect you. Leave the vengeance of your situation up to God and allow Him to intervene for you. We serve an incredible God who unconditionally loves us. He sent His only son to save us and He wants you in His family. He will bring divine retribution to those who have hurt you. Take heart in this today and cast out the lies of the enemy that tell you otherwise.

Pray for God to heal you and to restore your faith. We live in a fallen and broken world, but God can redeem you and your situation. If you're reading this today and have faced hurt or abuse, God is with you and He doesn't desire that for you. Have courage to seek God's protection and allow Him to heal you. He loves you so incredibly much! He will come to save you so have no fear. Take the steps towards freedom!

Prayer

Father, thank you for this courageous reminder today. I pray that You will save and protect me from my situation. I ask for Your divine retribution in my life. I know You see me and care about me. I pray that You would restore my fearful heart to You and heal my wounds. I ask for Your deliverance from fear and doubt. I come against the lies of the enemy that instill fear and I replace them with Your truth of Your love and ability to save. Thank you for loving and caring for me. In Jesus name, Amen.

Thoughts

You matter

five

Depression, Anxiety

This chapter is for those who are dealing with depression and anxiety. Depression and anxiety do not define you. God defines you. He chose for you to be here and He has a purpose for you. You may deal with depression or anxiety, but it is not your identity. It has no power over you. We all experience the feelings of depression and anxiety from time to time. The enemy will use lies to make us feel trapped in what we are feeling.

The truth in God's word reminds us that God is in control and has power in our lives. God can redeem and save us from these feelings. God also put godly counselors and mentors on this earth to walk us through these feelings. It's okay to seek help. Use the scriptures in this chapter to help you break off the lies of the enemy and seek out the appropriate help to overcome the struggles of depression and anxiety. God loves you and He cares for you so much. You are needed in this world and you can make a difference.

Scripture

"And we know that in all things God works for the good of those who love him, who have been called according to his purpose."

-Romans 8:28

Devotional

If you're feeling anxious today or feeling like things aren't going your way, remember this truth. We serve an incredible God who loves us so much. He works everything together for our good. We are all called to serve His purpose and if we put our focus on Him we will be able to see how well He leads us. Whatever your current situation may be, don't believe the lies the enemy tells you. Hold onto this truth that things will get better and God is moving on your behalf. It can be hard to see when the present looks dim, but our God cares so much more about you. He wants you to live your best life and serve Him.

Choose to speak life over yourself today and look for the good in everything. The enemy wants to keep you entrapped in the bondage of anxiety and depression, but God wants to set you free. Declare this truth and walk towards freedom. You have an incredible purpose for being here and God wants to show you that purpose. You will never be more fulfilled than when you're walking in God's purpose for your life. If you will seek Him, you'll begin to find that purpose and find freedom.

Prayer

Father, thank you for this truth today. I come against the lie of the enemy today and rebuke anxiety and depression from my life in the name of Jesus. I speak life over myself and declare that You have purpose and good things for my life. I pray that You would help me to overcome and see the good in every situation. Please help me through my current situation and to see the bright side. I thank You for never giving up on me even when I often give up myself. Help me to be strong. In Jesus name, Amen.

Thoughts

Scripture

"When I said, "My foot is slipping," Your unfailing love, Lord, supported me. When anxiety was great within me, your consolation brought me joy."

-Psalm 94:18-19

Devotional

If you're struggling today with anxiety or depression, hold onto this truth. God is with you and will support you, we just have to ask. He's available to console us through the hard times by bringing us joy. Joy isn't just a feeling we have, it can be a choice we make through God. God's love for us is unfailing which means He will never give up on us. It's important to declare and remember God's Truth when we are battling anxiety or depression because the world can become loud around us. It's easy to feel alone in your struggle, but God is with you and cares for you. He wants you to come to Him with your struggle and seek His help.

The biggest battle we face is believing the lies of the enemy. We have to seek God's truth to overcome. You are so precious to God and you are here for a purpose. He's ready to sweep you into His loving arms and bring you joy. Will you take a step towards God today? Will you make a move toward His joy and declare His truth? God is the only one who can bring us true freedom from our pain if we would only take a step toward Him. His truth can help us through the bad thoughts, the hard days and the darkest hours. Seek God today, friend, He's waiting.

Prayer

Father, thank you for this reminder today. I pray for the joy that only You can bring. I come against the lie of the enemy and rebuke anxiety and depression from my life. I speak life over myself and declare Your joy in my soul. I pray that You would help me to overcome the anxiety and depression so I can walk in Your freedom. Help me through this struggle and meet me where I'm at. I know my life is so precious to You. Help me to see myself through Your eyes. In Jesus name, Amen.

Thoughts

Scripture

"Praise be to the God and Father of our Lord Jesus Christ, the Father of compassion and the God of all comfort, who comforts us in all our troubles, so that we can comfort those in any trouble with the comfort we ourselves receive from God."

-2 Corinthians 1:3-4

Devotional

It can be the hardest to praise when we're feeling anxious or depressed. It can be hard to even pray, but those are the moments we have to push through and praise anyway. Don't believe the lie the enemy tells you and don't allow him to isolate you. In our hardest moments if we can find a way to pray and praise, we will begin to find freedom. When we bring our darkness into the light it begins to heal and fade. Declare this truth today and seek the comfort of our Heavenly Father. God sees you and wants the best for you. He has compassion for you and wants you to seek Him for healing.

The cloud of anxiety and depression can be heavy, but community can make a huge difference. God puts others in our community to help comfort us and offer compassion as well. Seek out the right community that will help you through your situation. Seek counseling or a godly mentor. Help others who are going through your same situation. Often times helping others will help us heal. Pray for God to put the right people in your path. Reach out to God and speak His truth over your life. When the lies get loud, tell yourself that you are a child of God, you have purpose and God loves you so incredibly much. He will help you through this season.

Prayer

Father, thank you for this truth today. I pray that You'll help me to overcome depression and anxiety and that You'll help me to see Your truth so clearly. I come against any lie of the enemy that tells me I'll never overcome. I declare Your truth in Jesus name that You are my comforter and through You I have freedom. Help me to find a solid community, mentor and counselor to help me find healing and freedom. Thank you for comforting me and having compassion for me. In Jesus name, amen.

Thoughts

Scripture

"I waited patiently for the Lord; he turned to me and heard my cry. He lifted me out of the slimy pit, out of the mud and mire; he set my feet on a rock and gave me a firm place to stand. He put a new song in my mouth, a hymn of praise to our God. Many will see and fear the Lord and put their trust in him."

-Psalm 40:1-3

Devotional

God hears your cry, friend. He knows how hard the situation is that you are going through today. Allow Him to set your feet on a rock and give you a new song. If you've been feeling the ups and downs that come with depression or anxiety, remember this truth today. God is here for you. He is moving in ways you may not see yet. Oftentimes when we're in a valley it's hard to see that we will ever get out of that place, but God promises to set us on a solid place. He is our rock and if we stand on His promises and truth we will begin to get out of that valley.

He is here to lift you out of the pit of anxiety and depression. Don't believe the lie of the enemy! God's truth is never failing. He has so much more for you. If we can learn to stand on His truth in the valley, it will be a foundation for us through all the ups and downs of life. God wants to give us a new song. A song of victory, freedom and truth! Begin to praise God even before you can see the promise come through. You'll begin to see His light and feel a lift from the place that feels heavy. Wait for God because His plans are greater!

Prayer

Father, thank you for this truth today. I stand firm on Your rock and declare Your praises over my life. I know that You are greater than any depression or anxiety I face. I pray that You would help me to walk in Your freedom and overcome the depression and anxiety. I come against the lie of the enemy in Jesus name and declare freedom and truth over my life. Thank you Lord for hearing my cry. I praise You Father and give You glory for the freedom found in You. You are so good Lord! In Jesus name, Amen.

Thoughts

Scripture

"The righteous cry out, and the Lord hears them; he delivers them from all their troubles. The Lord is close to the broken-hearted and saves those who are crushed in spirit."

-Psalm 34:17-18

Devotional

Friend, the Lord is close to you today. Don't believe any lie from the enemy that tells you anything different. God is here and saves those whose hearts are troubled or crushed. He's here to deliver you today and walk with you in freedom. He hears your every cry. He knows your every hurt. He holds every tear and wants you to turn toward Him. God is able to heal you and give you so much more than you can imagine. If you are experiencing depression or anxiety, seek Him today. Allow God to bring you a breath of fresh air.

When your situation seems impossible or you're feeling alone in your circumstances, call out to God. Trust Him with your heart today. Ask Him to deliver you and save you. He can lift your burden if you'll just ask Him. Try your hardest to look for the good and to focus your thoughts on God's Truth. Declare His truth over your life and situation continually. God's word has so much power and has the ability to turn your situation around if you'll lean into the truth.

Prayer

Father, thank you for this truth today. I ask that You would deliver me from my trouble and hear my cry. I ask that You would save me and be close to me. I come against the lie of the enemy in Jesus name and declare Your truth that You are with me and will deliver me. I pray that You'll help me to find freedom and overcome anxiety and depression. I ask that You would help me to lean into Your truth daily and help my thoughts to be pure and free from the lies of the enemy. In Jesus name, Amen.

Thoughts

Scripture

"Do not be anxious about anything, but in every situation, by prayer and petition, with thanksgiving, present your requests to God. And the peace of God, which transcends all understanding will guard your hearts and your minds in Christ Jesus. Finally, brothers and sisters, whatever is true, whatever is noble, whatever is right, whatever is pure, whatever is lovely, whatever is admirable- if anything is excellent or praiseworthy- think about such things."

-Philippians 4:6-8

Devotional

Our thoughts have the ability to control our lives, which is why it's so important for us to control our thoughts. If you are facing depression or anxiety, declare this truth today. This scripture reminds us in every situation to pray and give thanks to God. When we do this, we will have peace that will help us to guards our hearts and minds. This can be hard when you're experiencing depression or anxiety, but changing the way we think can help us find freedom. By praying, we are bringing our struggle out of the dark and making our requests known to God. By being thankful, we are reminding ourselves of what we do have instead of what we don't have. This helps us to see the light in our situation. It also let's God know how grateful we are for Him.

The second part of this verse holds so much power

for battling the lies of the enemy. It calls us to think on good things. If we allow our thoughts to dwell on the bad things we will go deeper down the hole of depression and anxiety. However, if we dwell on the good things we can begin to climb out of the hole and into God's light. We can begin to find freedom. It's a conscious habit and discipline to implement so we don't let our thoughts wander. Be disciplined today to think on good things and declare God's truth!

Prayer

Father, thank you for this truth today. I give You all the glory in my life. I'm thankful for all You've done and all You are going to do. I come against the lies of the enemy that have been holding me back in Jesus name and I declare Your truth over my life. I'm going to choose to think on good things. Help me to overcome the depression and anxiety and help me to be disciplined with my thought life. In Jesus name, amen.

Thoughts

Scripture

"Why, my soul, are you downcast? Why so disturbed within me? Put your hope in God, for I will yet praise him, my Savior and my God."

-Psalm 42:11

Devotional

Sometimes we have to do some self-talk to find our way out of our current situation. If you're experiencing depression or anxiety today, remember this truth to put your hope in God. It can be hard to hope when you don't see what the future holds. We have to hope anyways and believe that God has a better plan for us. We have to praise God in our storm and declare His truth. Sometimes that takes a little discipline to remind ourselves of God's power. It helps us to declare His truth and take control of our thought life to think on good things.

Hope is a feeling of expectation for the future and a trust that God will work things out. When going through a hard season that brings the feeling of depression or anxiety, we have to put our hope in God. We have to believe and trust God has a greater plan and will bring us through this. We have to praise Him when it hurts and know that He is moving on our behalf. We have to remember our purpose and remember that God put us here on this earth to make a difference. You've got this, friend! Keep hoping and keep leaning on God. Keep declaring His truth over your life to overcome the lies!

Prayer

Father, thank you for this truth today. I pray that You would restore my hope in You and in my future. I come against the lies of the enemy in Jesus name and proclaim Your truth of hope over my life. I praise You for all You do in my life. You are a good father and I know You have good plans for my life. Help me to overcome the lies of depression and anxiety and to walk in Your freedom. Thank you, God, for the purpose You have for me. In Jesus name, amen.

Thoughts

You are enough

Six

Insecurity, Shame, Comparison

This chapter is for overcoming insecurity, shame, comparison and any of the feelings associated with these topics. These topics are often buried in our lives as lies we don't easily like to talk about. It can be difficult to admit any insecurity or shame in our life. It can also be hard to admit when we compare.

However, it's important to recognize the lies so that we can overcome them with God's truth. I believe we have all struggled with these things at some point as they show up in multiple ways in our lives. You can have freedom over this today in Jesus name as you read through each scripture by declaring God's truth.

Scripture

"Who then is the one who condemns? No one. Christ Jesus who died- more than that, who was raised to life- is at the right hand of God and is also interceding for us."

-Romans 8:34

Devotional

If you're feeling shameful today or full of regret from your past, know that God isn't condemning you. In fact, God wants to forgive you and intercede on your behalf. There's a big difference between conviction and condemnation. Conviction is when we know in our heart we shouldn't do something and seek forgiveness or resist the temptation. Condemnation is from the enemy and puts shame on us for sinning. The enemy often tempts us into doing things we shouldn't and immediately switches gears by heaping shame over us for sinning. However, God loves us and wants the best for us. God is waiting with open arms to forgive us.

Shame can show itself in many forms in our lives. You might have heard the phrase growing up, "Shame on you," but God is here saying, "Shame off you." If God Himself doesn't condemn us, then we shouldn't let anyone else do it either. When you give it to God, He gives you freedom. Jesus is at His right-hand interceding on your behalf. He's sitting there telling our Father that He understands and knows what it's like to be in your situation. He's on your side and so is God. Jesus came to earth to pay for our sin and He has faced everything we could ever possibly face. Whatever you're dealing with today, declare God's truth over yourself knowing that you are not condemned or shamed.

Prayer

Father, thank you for Your truth today. I pray that You will help me to lean on You and that You will search my heart and forgive me for anything unpleasing to You. Holy Spirit, please convict me and help me to move forward from the things holding me back. Jesus, I know You intercede on my behalf and I thank you that I can relate to You. Thank you for paying for my sin on the cross. I pray that You would remove the lies of shame that I'm feeling today and replace it with Your truth and love. In Jesus name, Amen.

Thoughts

Scripture

"And the prayer offered in faith will make the sick person well; the Lord will raise them up. If they have sinned, they will be forgiven. Therefore confess your sins to each other and pray for each other so that you may be healed. The prayer of a righteous person is powerful and effective."

-James 5:15-16

Devotional

If you're feeling alone in your problems or like you can't talk to anyone about what's going on, apply this scripture to your life. We shouldn't face life alone. We need community we can trust and rely on no matter what. There's healing found by confessing to each other in godly community and praying through our problems. Seek godly wisdom today and talk with a trusted mentor or friend. These verses in James hold so much truth when we are facing insecurities, comparison or shame. God's forgiveness is always available and when we talk with a trusted friend about our troubles, we begin to see the light at the end of the tunnel. We have to bring our feelings and problems into the light for the darkness to be healed. The enemy doesn't want anyone to know about what you are dealing with, which keeps it in the dark.

We also need to pray about what we are facing. Prayer is so powerful and we need to make it our first response rather than a last result. God hears every prayer no matter how small, big or impossible it may seem. He just wants you to talk with Him and lean on Him. He cares about every aspect of your life. Your prayers hold so much power. Whatever lie you are believing, hold onto this truth today that you can overcome through Christ and community.

Prayer

Father, I come to You right now and ask You to help me through my current situation. I'm declaring light over the darkness and asking for Your healing power. I know there is power in prayer and You care about me so much. I pray that You will help me find trusted community to walk through my situation so I can find full freedom. Thank you for Your word today. In Jesus Name, Amen.

Thoughts

Scripture

"For God so loved the world that he gave his one and only Son, that whoever believes in him shall not perish but have eternal life. For God did not send his Son into the world to condemn the world, but to save the world through him."

-John 3:16-17

Devotional

This verse is widely known because it holds so much truth. No matter what you may be facing, you can always rely on God's truth to overcome. When you begin to doubt and those feelings of insecurity, shame or comparison arise, remember what God says about you. He loved you so incredibly much that He gave His only Son for you to find freedom. This means we no longer have to pay for our sin ourselves, we just have to accept Jesus as our Savior. Shame and insecurity have no place in our lives because Jesus saved us from it. This is available to everyone, so never believe the lie that you don't qualify.

God wants intimacy with you and He chooses not to remember your sin. Jesus made the ultimate sacrifice to save us and all He wants in return is our love and commitment through relationship. Often times culture places shame on us, brings out insecurity and blames religion. We live in a world where our lives are highlighted on social media for all to see. This can cause us to feel comparison or shame if our lives don't look a certain way. It can also cause us to feel like we aren't good enough for God's love, however this verse proves that God loves you. He wants to save you and give you eternal life! When we know this truth about God, we can overcome the lie of the enemy.

Prayer

Father, thank you for Your Son, Jesus, dying on the cross for my sins. I'm so grateful that You don't condemn me and that You remove all shame, insecurity and comparison from my thoughts. I come against the lie of the enemy that says I don't qualify for Your forgiveness and I replace it with the truth that Jesus saved me by grace through faith. Please help me to see myself through Your eyes and to accept Your love. Thank you, Jesus, for being my Savior. In Jesus name, Amen.

Thoughts

Scripture

"We do not dare to classify or compare ourselves with some who commend themselves. When they measure themselves by themselves, they are not wise. We, however, will not boast beyond proper limits, but will confine our boasting to the sphere of service God himself has assigned us, a sphere that also includes you."

-2 Corinthians 10:12-13

Devotional

This verse shows us when we compare ourselves it's not wise. Comparison brings out things God didn't intend us to feel and it makes us feel worse about ourselves. When we compare our life, it disvalues who God created us to be because He intentionally crafted us. We have to remember our value and who God created us to be rather than wishing to be like someone else. This can be hard when we face comparison every time we get on social media. It's something we have to be conscious of and constantly remind ourselves of God's truth.

Comparison tends to rob us of our calling by causing us to focus on everyone else's calling. In the context of this verse, boasting doesn't mean to brag or to selfishly promote ourselves rather it means to have a godly confidence. If we have a godly confidence in who God created us to be then we won't bother in comparing ourselves. It humbles us and keeps us grounded when we keep our focus on God. All we do should give glory to God rather than ourselves. When we remember this, we are more focused on His purpose than our own. God also gives us each a sphere of service (or influence) where we can make a difference for Him. If we're too busy comparing our sphere to someone else's, we will miss the opportunity that God has for us. Take time to evaluate your heart today and seek God through this truth to overcome the lie of comparison.

Prayer

Father, thank you for who You created me to be. Thank you for thinking of me and for creating me with a purpose. I pray that You'll help me to overcome the comparison in my life. I pray that You will help me to have a godly confidence in my identity in You and the sphere of influence You gave me. I pray that You will help me to steward the gift well that You've given me to use and to influence the people You've put in my circle. Help me to keep my eyes on You. In Jesus name, Amen.

Thoughts

Scripture

"Each one should test their own actions. Then they can take pride in themselves alone, without comparing themselves to someone else, for each one should carry their own load."

-Galatians 6:4-5

Devotional

If you find yourself comparing today, remember the truth in this verse. God calls us to test our own actions, meaning that we should weigh ourselves against His truth about how we should live. When we test our own actions, we can know that we are acting purely in who God created us to be. We can be real, honest and operate in our own gifts rather than trying to be like someone else. By testing our actions, we can also make sure that we are doing things for the right reasons. Often times comparison can cause us to pursue things with the wrong intentions. It can also cause us to spend money we don't need to spend or filter our lives a certain way to the world. God has so much more for you and created you with everything you need to live out your unique calling with your gifts.

We're meant to carry our own gifts and live out the purpose God has for us. We have to run in our own lane and be confident in everything God has given us, not what He's given others. If we start to focus on what others have been gifted with, then we lose sight of our own lane. We may unknowingly begin to carry the load of someone else's calling instead of our own. We have to remind ourselves of the load God's given us to carry. We have to be grateful for our calling and focus on our own lane. We have to persevere in our purpose. When we persevere, we can then help others because we're operating in the identity God's given us.

Prayer

Father, thank you for the calling You've given me. Test my actions and create in me a pure heart. Help me to carry my own load and not lose sight of the calling You've given me. Help me to run confidently in the lane You've given me and to persevere in my calling. Help me to encourage others in their calling. I come against the lie of comparison that says I'm not good enough and I replace it with the truth that you've created me with everything for my calling. In Jesus name, Amen.

Thoughts

Scripture

"Do not be afraid; you will not be put to shame. Do not fear disgrace; you will not be humiliated. You will forget the shame of your youth and remember no more the reproach of your widowhood."

-Isaiah 54:4

Devotional

If you are feeling insecure or shame today, remember this truth that God gives us. We are told not to fear. We're not put to shame by God. The world may make us feel that way, but it doesn't hold truth in God's word. God doesn't put shame or humiliation on us. We may have experienced shame in our past or our youth, but God's word tells us to not remember it. Growing up you may have had negative words spoken over you that hurt. I want you to know that's not who you are and that's not what God thinks of you. He loves you so incredibly much! You can overcome the lies of shame you may have felt throughout your youth by holding onto this scripture.

This verse goes on and refers to widowhood in the sense of a season of desolation, loneliness, or lack. This verse tells us not to remember the reproach that came with that season. This could be a number of things that come to mind when you reflect on life. God is saying not to hold that against yourself. He forgives you and chooses not to remember your past so you shouldn't remember it either. All we can do is learn from our past and move on. You are not your past. Wherever you are today, rest in the truth that God doesn't put shame or insecurity on you. We can hold onto His truth today.

Prayer

Father, thank you for this truth today that You don't put shame on me. I'm thankful that I can walk confidently in Your truth today. Help me to rest in this truth today and not to fear. Help me to overcome the lies with Your truth. Help me to walk in freedom and not to hold my past against myself. Thank you that Your Son died on the cross to forgive me of my sin and that You choose to remember it no more. In Jesus name, Amen.

Thoughts

Scripture

"Therefore, put on the full armor of God, so that when the day of evil comes, you may be able to stand your ground, and after you have done everything, to stand. Stand firm then, with the belt of truth buckled around your waist, with the breastplate of righteousness in place, and with your feet fitted with the readiness that comes from the gospel of peace. In addition to all this, take up the shield of faith, with which you can extinguish all the flaming arrows of the evil one. Take the helmet of salvation and the sword of the Spirit, which is the word of God."

-Ephesians 6:13-17

Devotional

If you're facing insecurity, comparison or feeling shame today, pray for God's full armor. This verse reminds us of the protection God gives us in His truth. When we put on the full armor of God, we are putting on His truth to fight against the lies. The preceding scripture talks about what we are fighting against. It's not just flesh and bones, but spirits and principalities. There's a very real enemy who only wants you to hear the lies spoken over your life. However, God wants you to know and walk confidently in His truth. When we pray for the armor of God, we are spiritually suiting up and protecting ourselves.

It's a constant fight, but one worth fighting for every day. God's spiritual armor covers us from head to toe and reminds us to stand firm in His truth. There's so much power in God's truth and authority in Jesus' name. We have to use this to fight the battles we face every day and remember our strength comes from God. When we remember God's truth, we can fight off the lie of insecurity, shame and comparison. We can remember who God says we are and rest in His presence.

Prayer

Father, thank you for this truth today. I pray that You'll equip me today and every day with the full armor of God. I pray that You will help me to put this truth into action and to fight off the lies of insecurity, shame and comparison. I pray that You will protect me today and guard my heart and mind. Help me to hide Your word in my heart. In Jesus name, Amen.

Thoughts

You have hope

seven

Hopelessness, Discouragement, Disappointment

This chapter is for those who are feeling hopeless, discouraged or disappointed. You may have been hurt by someone, missed out on an opportunity, or experienced a loss. The list could go on. Whatever you are facing today, there is hope to be found in Jesus. You can't believe the lie of the enemy that causes you to doubt. God has incredible plans for you.

Though we live in a fallen world, you can be a light for God in the broken places. We can use our disappointments to help another person. When we overcome the lies, we can begin to see opportunities to share hope with others. The enemy is here to steal our hope but God wants to redeem our situation. Trust God to help you overcome with His truth today.

Scripture

"May the God of hope fill you with all joy and peace as you trust in him, so that you may overflow with hope by the power of the Holy Spirit."

-Romans 15:13

Devotional

If you're feeling hopelessness or discouraged, remember this truth. We serve the God of hope. He is able to restore our hope and fill us with joy and peace. He just asks that we trust Him. This can be hard when we don't see where our situation is going, but it's the first step toward renewed hope. The closer we get to God, the more we will begin to trust Him with every aspect of our lives. When we are close to the Father, we will begin to reach new levels of hope, joy and peace. God wants to fill us, we just have to seek Him.

The more we seek God and declare His truth in our life, the more we will fill ourselves with His hope. We have to declare this truth to overcome the lies of hopelessness the enemy tries to tells us. We have to walk in truth so that we can be full with God's love and truth. The Holy Spirit lives inside of you and will give you power to overflow that love to others. When we live from a place of overflow we are able to give so much more. Just like a cup that you run water in until it spills over. We can be full and give at the same time. Our hope will spill over to help others find God's hope!

Prayer

Father, thank you for this reminder today. I pray that You would help me to be filled with hope, joy and peace. I come against the lie of the enemy that steals my hope in Jesus name and declare Your hope in my life. I pray for the power of the Holy Spirit to overflow hope from my life. I ask for deliverance from any hopelessness in my life and pray for freedom so that I can have restored hope. I ask that You would help me to live from a place of overflow so I can help others find hope as well. In Jesus name, Amen.

Thoughts

Scripture

"Have I not commanded you? Be strong and courageous. Do not be afraid; do not be discouraged, for the Lord your God will be with you wherever you go."

-Joshua 1:9

Devotional

If you're feeling discouraged today, declare this truth over your life. Choose to be strong and courageous. Remember that God is with you wherever you go. He has a plan even if you can't see it right now. Whenever you're feeling discouraged or disappointed trust that God will come through for you. Begin to step out in faith and choose to see the good things happening in your life. Choose to be thankful for what you do have and trust that God has a plan.

It can be hard to see God's plan when something doesn't work out the way we thought it would, but we have to remember He has good plans for our lives. Sometimes we may think something is right for us, but God has the whole picture. He knows exactly where we need to be and He sees things we don't see. We have to keep moving forward and we can't allow discouragement or disappointment to paralyze us. The enemy wants us to stay in this place of discouragement, but God's truth commands us to be strong. God wants freedom for us and wants us to keep moving forward!

Prayer

Father, thank you for this truth today. I pray You would help me to be strong and courageous today. I ask for Your help to overcome the discouragement and that I would begin to see You in everything I do. I come against the lie of the enemy that discourages me in Jesus name and I proclaim Your truth today that You are with me everywhere I go. I pray that You would restore my hope and help me to see Your truth. In Jesus name, Amen.

Thoughts

Scripture

"Trust in the Lord with all your heart and lean not on your own understanding; in all your ways submit to him, and he will make your paths straight."

-Proverbs 3:5-6

Devotional

When we are experiencing hopelessness, discouragement or disappointment it can be hard to trust in the things we don't see. Hold onto this truth today and declare it over your life. Choose to trust God and lean on Him. We may not understand everything that is going on in our lives, but we have to trust that God is moving. We have to trust that He will work it all for our good. He has a plan for your life and you just have to submit to Him. This can be hard to do when we think we know what is best for our lives. God knows our whole situation and He already knows the best path for us. We just have to trust and follow Him.

When we follow God, He will make our path straight. It's like when you go hiking without a map or directions, you may get discouraged because you don't know which way to go. When you go hiking with a GPS or map, it will guide you step by step. You may not be able to see what's fully ahead, but each step will get you there. Just like we trust our map for the right path, we have to trust that God is taking us on the best path possible. We have to trust with our whole heart 100%.

Prayer

Father, thank you for this reminder today. I pray that You would help me to fully trust You with my entire heart. I ask that You would lead me on the best path for my life. I surrender fully to You. I come against any lie of the enemy in Jesus name and proclaim Your truth over my life. I know You have good plans for me and that You will guide me. Thank you for Your wisdom and guidance. In Jesus name, amen.

Thoughts

Scripture

"I have told you these things, so that in me you may have peace. In this world you will have trouble. But take heart! I have overcome the world."

-John 16:33

Devotional

We live in a fallen world that's full of trouble and we have to make sure we aren't putting our hope in this world. We have to put our hope in Jesus! That's the only way we will ever have peace in this world and be able to have hope. Jesus has overcome the world so we don't have to worry. It can be hard to have hope when you see the current news and see the struggles in the world. We have to focus on God and seek Him in the difficult times. We have to declare this truth to overcome the lie of the enemy that tells us there's no hope.

The enemy doesn't want us to bring the hope of Jesus to the world, but we have to speak against those lies and remember this truth. God needs us to shine our light to the world through Jesus. When we have hope, others will see the light in our lives and begin to want that as well. We have a mission to share the hope of Jesus with the world. We all have a sphere of influence where we can do this and we can't let the enemy steal that influence from us by stealing our hope. Walk in this truth today!

Prayer

Father, thank you for this truth today. I pray that You would help me to have hope even when the world looks dark. Help me to share Your hope with others and to be a light for You. I come against any lie of the enemy that says there is no hope and I declare Your truth in Jesus name that You have overcome the world. You have authority in my life and I proclaim Your hope and truth. I ask that You would help me when times are hard to remember Your truth and to have hope. In Jesus name, Amen.

Thoughts

Scripture

"*We are hard pressed on every side, but not crushed; perplexed, but not in despair; persecuted, but not abandoned, struck down, but not destroyed.*"

-2 Corinthians 4:8-9

Devotional

You may find yourself in the valley today, unsure of how you'll get out, but remember this truth. No matter your situation, God is right there with you. It will get better. We can have hope because of this truth today. We will not be crushed, abandoned or destroyed! We have victory in Jesus name! When life is putting pressure on you and the enemy is whispering lies that you won't get out of this place, declare God's Truth. This is only a season and God is here to help you through it.

Stay strong by leaning on God's word and diving into His presence. Draw near to God in the hard situations and you'll begin to see Him moving on your behalf. As we grow closer to the Lord, we'll begin to trust Him more and see His goodness more. Your situation is not hopeless. God has a plan for your life and He will make a way. Don't allow yourself to be crushed or struck down. Rise up and walk in the freedom found in God's Truth.

Prayer

Father, thank you for this truth today. I pray that You would help me to see Your truth in every situation. I proclaim today that I am an overcomer and I won't be crushed. I come against any lie of the enemy in Jesus name that tells me otherwise and I declare Your truth over my life that I will not be struck down. I ask for Your guidance, wisdom and protection over my life. I pray for renewed hope and restored faith in You. In Jesus name, Amen.

Thoughts

Scripture

"*But those who hope in the Lord will renew their strength. They will soar on wings like eagles; they will run and not grow weary, they will walk and not be faint.*"

-Isaiah 40:31

Devotional

If you're feeling hopeless or discouraged, remember this truth. We have to put our hope in the Lord and He will renew our strength. That means instead of putting hope in our situation or future desires, we surrender it to God and put our hope in Him. He already knows your deepest dreams and desires. We have to trust that God will take care of our every need. When our hope is in God, everything will fall into place just as He planned. We have to overcome the lie the enemy tells us our hope is in our desires, our things and the world. Our hope is directly in God to provide our desires, provision and future for us. We have to declare God's truth to remind ourselves where our hope is found.

When we put our hope in God, we will soar like wings on eagles, we won't grow weary and we won't be faint. How incredible is this?! God will do incredible things in our lives when our hope is in Him because we will be focused on His will. When we focus on God, we will begin to see His goodness more in our lives because we are trusting in Him. Whatever you focus on is where your heart and hope will be. When we put our hope in God and keep our eyes on Him we begin to see through His lens. This is how we live a life full of hope and wonder!

Prayer

Father, thank you for this truth today. I pray that You would help me to put my hope in You. I come against any lie of the enemy today that tells me my hope is in this world and I declare Your truth that my hope is in You. I pray that You would help me to soar with You and trust You. I pray that You would help my focus to stay on You especially when life gets hard. In Jesus name, Amen.

Thoughts

Scripture

"Hope deferred makes the heart sick, but a longing fulfill is a tree of life."

-Proverbs 13:12

Devotional

Hope is a funny thing. It's something we constantly face whether it's getting our hopes up for something or getting let down when things don't turn out how we hoped they would. I misunderstood true hope for so long. As I've faced disappointment and the feeling of hope being dashed, I began to realize I didn't understand true hope. Hope is not in the things we see. Hope is not a wish, it's a will- God's will. Hope is in the unseen things and having a confident expectation that God is moving. Hope is trusting God for that promise even when it seems impossible and hope is still trusting Him even if it doesn't look how we thought it would.

When we have hope for something and that something either doesn't happen, gets delayed or goes a different direction it causes heartache. When it happens over and over again it's like our heart becomes sick and it's hard to hope. Our hope can't be in what we are hoping for, but rather our hope has to be in God and He will fulfill our desires. God knows our future better than anyone. He knows the perfect timing, every part of the scenario. He knows the current state of our heart and mind. He also knows when we need protecting as situations change. We can overcome the heartache of deferred hope by trusting God and having an expectation in His goodness. When we embrace God's goodness we can share that with others to help them find hope. Trust God today and put your hope in Him!

Prayer

Father, thank you for the hope that only You provide. Thank you for the plans You have for me and thank you for seasons of wilderness where I grow to know you more closely. Thank you for restoring my hope through You. I ask You continue to encourage me through hope, joy and love and renew my strength. I come against the lies of the enemy today that steal and discourage my hope and I declare Your truth over my life that I can put my hope in you. In Jesus name, Amen.

Thoughts

God's got you

eight

Finance, Provision

This chapter is for those struggling with their finances or to trust God for provision. One of the greatest lies of the enemy is around money. There is a spirit of mammon (love of money) that we face throughout life. Satan will use it to make us question God's provision and goodness. He will even stir us to be independent from God.

Money can cause us stress, heartache, fear and pride. Money itself isn't bad, but the love of money can destroy our lives. That's why we need to understand God's truth about finances. We have to understand that we are merely stewards of the money in our lives and that God is our provider. When we understand what God says on the matter of money, we can overcome the lies of the enemy.

Scripture

"Therefore I tell you, do not worry about your life, what you will eat or drink; or about your body, what you will wear. Is not life more than food, and the body more than clothes? Look at the birds of the air; they do not sow or reap or store away in barns, and yet your heavenly Father feeds them. Are you not much more valuable than they? Can any one of you by worrying add a single hour to your life?... But seek first his kingdom and his righteousness, and all these things will be given to you as well."

-Matthew 6:25-27; 33

Devotional

If you are struggling with your finances or trusting God for your provision, hold onto this truth today. God will provide for you. He cares about every living creature and cares even more for you. We see right here in this verse just how much He cares for us. He doesn't want us to worry about anything. I've always heard the saying that worrying is like sitting in a rocking chair, it gives you something to do, but gets you nowhere. That's so true. Worrying about our situation won't add anything but stress to our lives. God will provide everything we need. It may not look how we thought it would or be in our timing but it will be everything we need and more.

We may not understand how or why God does things the way He does but He always comes through for us. Our job is to continually seek Him first and trust Him. One way to do this is by thanking Him for what we have in our current season. This helps us to refocus and not worry as much about what we don't have yet. God knows our value and He knows how to care for us. Whatever lie the enemy has tried to tell you, hold onto God's truth today. He sees you and He's working on your provision!

Prayer

Father, thank you for this truth today. I pray that You would help me to trust You for my provision. I ask that You would financially provide for my current needs. I come against any lie from the enemy that tells me You won't come through and I declare Your truth right now that You will provide. Thank you for everything You have provided so far in my life. I'm so grateful for You Lord. In Jesus name, amen.

Thoughts

Scripture

"The Lord is my shepherd, I lack nothing. He makes me lie down in green pastures, he leads me beside quiet waters, he refreshes my soul. He guides me along the right paths for his names sake. Even though I walk through the darkest valley, I will fear no evil, for you are with me; your rod and staff, they comfort me. You prepare a table before me in the presence of my enemies. You anoint my head with oil; my cup overflows. Surely your goodness and love will follow me all the days of my life, and I will dwell in the house of the Lord forever."

-Psalm 23

Devotional

When you are stressed about your finances and feel like God isn't coming through for you, remember this verse. While it may be hard to believe, we don't actually lack anything. God provides us with all we need and whatever our current season may hold, He gives us exactly what we need. The enemy will try to convince you that God doesn't provide and that God isn't good, but this truth tells us God is good. Whenever those lies start to flood our mind, remember this truth and speak it over yourself. No matter what we walk through, God is with us. His goodness and love will follow us.

I know it can be hard when you are struggling with where you're at in this season. You may be struggling to make ends meet or have fallen on a financial hardship. God sees. He knows and He is working behind the scenes. He will come through and just wants you to trust Him. Lean on God for His provision and see what can be learned through this season. He will guide you and refresh you. He will guide your path. Choose to trust God through this season and believe He will come through. Do all that you can and trust God with the rest.

Prayer

Father, thank you for this sweet reminder. I pray that You would walk with me and help me to see Your hand of provision in my life. I ask for Your provision in my current situation. I come against any lie from the enemy that says You aren't providing and declare Your truth over my life that You always provide for me. I know You are my shepherd and You are my provider. Thank you for Your provision. In Jesus name, Amen.

Thoughts

Scripture

"I lift my eyes to the mountains- where does my help come from? My help comes from the Lord, the Maker of heaven and earth. He will not let your foot slip- he who watches over you will not slumber."

-Psalm 121:1-3

Devotional

So often we can forget where our help truly comes from when our current circumstances are dim. We can get caught up in the hustle of the world and strive to provide for ourselves without seeking God's help. When we start to get stressed over our finances or provision, we need to remember this truth. Our help comes from God. He is always looking out for us and is with us. He will come through and will make a way. Trust Him to provide for you. Don't believe the lies that this world tells you about having to do it all yourself.

God wants us to lean on Him for help. He says He won't let our foot slip. God will make a way where there was no way. We just have to ask and trust. We have to know that whatever our current situation is will be okay even if it doesn't look like it will. We also have to be thankful for what we have. When your situation seems impossible, give it to God. He cares so much more than you may ever realize. God isn't sleeping on the job, He's working on your behalf at all times.

Prayer

Father, thank you for Your help. I know my help comes from You and I come against any lie of the enemy that tells me my help comes from this world. I know You will provide because Your Truth tells me You are my provider. I ask for Your help through my current situation and that You will help me through it. Give me hope when it seems too dark. I trust You to come through. Thank you for Your provision. In Jesus name, Amen.

Thoughts

Scripture

"Keep your lives free from the love of money and be content with what you have, because God has said, "Never will I leave you; never will I forsake you.""

-Hebrews 13:5

Devotional

It's easy to get caught up in comparison and look at all that others have especially when we're struggling with what we don't have. In those moments we can easily begin to love money because of what it can do for our current situation. We have to remember that our help comes from God and that He will provide all we need. It's important to focus on contentment in our current situation and trust God so that we don't give into the lie of the enemy. God's truth tells us that He will never leave us or forsake us. He isn't going to leave us high and dry where we are in our situation.

The enemy will lie and tell us that money is the only solution for our problems, but this scripture overcomes that lie. God is the solution to our every problem and He is our provider. Hold onto this truth when your situation becomes overwhelming. Begin to lean on God to provide for you and trust that He will do what He says. Embrace God's love and trust His timing for His provision. You will make it. God sees you where you are. He's moving in ways you can't even see to provide for you.

Prayer

Father, thank you for Your provision. I come against any love of money in my life and any lie that the enemy has told me and I speak Your truth that You are my provider in Jesus name. I know that You will come through in my current situation. I ask that You would help me to be content where You have me and not to worry about my situation. You are so good to me. Thank you. In Jesus name, Amen.

Thoughts

It is Written

"But blessed is the one who trusts in the Lord, whose confidence is in him. They will be like a tree planted by the water that sends out its roots into the stream. It does not fear when heat comes; its leaves are always green. It has not worries in a year of drought and never fails to bear fruit."

-Jeremiah 17:7-8

Devotional

Life is so much better when we trust in God for our provision. It takes the pressure off of us when we realize our place and God's place. It's up to us to do what we can and to trust God to do the rest. If you're struggling to trust Him with your finances or provision, hold onto this truth. When we trust God to provide we are like a tree planted by the water. When a tree is by the water, its roots are next to its source. This is like us when we stay close to the Father, who is our source. We will trust His provision more and see it more clearly.

It's easy to believe the lies of the enemy and get out of focus. We have to overcome the lie with this truth. Let's focus on constantly staying connected to our true source in God. Let's continually feed ourselves with God's truth. This will help when we are struggling through our current season by focusing on God. It will also help our confidence to be in God rather than in the world or our job or our relationships. We will begin to stress less and trust God more.

Prayer

Father, thank you for this truth today. I pray that You will help me to put my trust in You rather than my circumstances. I know my confidence is in You. I come against any lie that tells me otherwise and declare Your truth in Jesus name. I ask that You would help me to be planted closely to You like the tree by the water. I ask for Your provision in my situation and that You would help me through it. Thank you. In Jesus name, Amen.

Thoughts

Scripture

"Remember this: Whoever sows sparingly will also reap sparingly, and whoever sows generously will also reap generously. Each of you should give what you have decided in your heart to give, not reluctantly or under compulsion, for God loves a cheerful giver. And God is able to bless you abundantly, so that in all things at all times, having all that you need, you will abound in every good work."

-2 Corinthians 9:6-8

Devotional

God calls us to live generously. This doesn't always mean in your finances, but in your time, your skills, and your life. Whatever you are able to give, do so generously. God doesn't want us to give reluctantly or out of guilt because then it's not truly from the heart. Living generously can be hard when we don't have much to give. Don't let the enemy tell you the lie that you have nothing to give. Even if you can't be generous financially, you are made with specific gifts to pour into others. So, give your life abundantly in serving God. God will provide for your every need so focus on serving Him. Don't serve Him to get something from Him, but because He already gives us everything.

Generosity can be hard to think about when we feel like God isn't providing for us. It can be hard to help others when we need help ourselves. The enemy wants us to be self-focused, but God calls us to put our focus toward Heaven. God will bless you and will give you all you need and more. Our success isn't measured by how much we make, or what's in our bank account. Our success is measured by the difference we are able to make for God while on earth. So, when times are tough, focus on others and watch what God will do.

Prayer

Father, thank you for reminding me to be generous. Thank you for Your truth today. Please help me to live more generously. I come against any lie of the enemy that causes me to worry or be selfish and I speak truth that I will live generously and love others more. I pray that You would provide financially for me and that You would bless me so I can bless others. In Jesus name, Amen.

Thoughts

Scripture

"And my God will meet all your needs according to the riches of his glory in Christ Jesus."

-Philippians 4:19

Devotional

If you are feeling forgotten in your situation today, remember this truth. God will meet all of your needs. He is your provider for every situation. It can be hard to wait on the provision you've been praying for and the enemy will lie to us to make us believe it will never happen. Whatever need you have today, God hears you and He's working on it for you. His timing is perfect. We just have to trust that He will fulfill His promises. He wants good things for our lives. We have to try our best not to stress when things look impossible.

Don't believe the lies the enemy tries to tell you about your provision and current situation. Hold onto the truth that God provides and will meet your needs. God has already done so much in our lives. He gave us the greatest gift in Jesus. We no longer have to pay for our sin when we accept Jesus in our hearts because Jesus gave His life to save us. If God provided a Savior, He will certainly provide for your needs. He didn't bring you this far just to leave you on your own. Lean into God's truth and trust Him through the waiting.

Prayer

Father, thank you for meeting my every need. I know that You will provide and I trust Your timing. I come against the lie of the enemy that says I'm never going to get out of my current financial situation and I proclaim God's provision over my life in Jesus name. I know You're moving in ways that I can't yet see and I trust You to come through for me. Thank you for all that You've already provided me. In Jesus name, Amen.

Thoughts

You are set free

nine

Control. Humility. Stress

This chapter is for when you're feeling overly busy, stressed and like you have to constantly be in control for life to go right. Any perfectionists relate? The enemy will lie to us to make us believe if we aren't hustling or constantly doing more that we will miss out. I believe we have all experienced this at some point whether we're in school or in our jobs. The world is a competitive place that drives this mentality to hustle.

The struggle can be so real, but we have to seek after what God tells us. I once heard a pastor say, "If the Devil can't make you bad, he'll make you busy." When we are overly busy it distracts us from doing the things that God has created us to do. It also just wears us out physically and emotionally. As you read through this chapter, I pray that you will be able to recognize the lies from the enemy in your life and overcome with God's truth.

Scripture

"Come to me, all you who are weary and burdened, and I will give you rest. Take my yoke upon you and learn from me, for I am gentle and humble in heart, and you will find rest for your souls. For my yoke is easy and my burden is light."

-Matthew 11:28-30

Devotional

If you are feeling stressed today, give it to Jesus. He can handle it. This scripture is a beautiful reminder that when we come to Jesus and give our worries, stress, and burdens to Him then we will find true rest. Often, we may feel in those moments of stress that we have to fix it ourselves or deal with it on our own. First, we have to come to Jesus. It doesn't say "after you fix everything" or "after you get to a certain spiritual level," it just says come and it says all, meaning everyone can come to Him.

Secondly, to find rest we have to take His yoke upon ourselves and learn from Him. Yokes were used in the fields for oxen. The oxen were paired together by a device called a yoke. By taking on the yoke of Jesus, it's a way of submitting to God and learning from Him. The scripture also says you will find rest for your souls. Our souls carry all our thoughts and emotion. We are made up of body, soul and spirit. Each have an important role and it specifically says rest for your souls. We have to give our feelings to God and accept His rest. Often times the biggest area of rest we need is from being emotionally exhausted.

Finally, it says...His yoke is easy and burden is light. This expresses God's character. His character isn't heavy or harsh, but light and easy. If we submit to God and surrender our troubles to Him, He will give us the rest we so desperately need.

Prayer

Father, I admit I'm not great at resting and fully submitting to You. When I'm stressed and worn out, I need Your help to rest and I submit myself to You daily. Show me how to fully rest in Your presence and how to partner with You. I come against the lie of busyness in Jesus name and I replace it with Your truth of rest. I fully trust You and I know You can handle every aspect of my life. Thank you for the rest You are giving me. In Jesus name, Amen

Thoughts

Scripture

"He has shown you, O mortal, what is good. And what does the LORD require of you? To act justly and to love mercy and to walk humbly with your God."

-Micah 6:8

Devotional

Often times we can feel stressed and heavy from trying to control everything in our lives. Sometimes we don't realize we are trying to do it all ourselves. This is a great verse to teach us to lean on God and give it all to Him. In this verse we see God has already shown us all we need to live our best life. In the context of this verse, the Israelites are being instructed to turn back to God as they have a habit of doing life in their own power rather than through God's power. We have to be willing to let go of control and surrender in humility to God. We can do this through acting justly (doing good to others), loving mercy (having compassion on others) and walking humbly with God (submitting everything to God and being willing to walk alongside Him rather than run ahead in our own strength).

This is easier said than done, but focus on these three areas each day by praying this verse and you'll find yourself releasing the pressure of having to figure everything out yourself. God has so much more for you. All you have to do is just surrender to His will. He longs to give you the desires of your heart. When we seek

Him, our desires align with His desires and plans for our lives. God has always had a plan for your life so you can trust Him by giving Him control. Take the pressure off yourself and allow God to walk with you.

Prayer

Father, I surrender control to You today and humble myself before You. I pray that You will help me to act justly, love mercy and walk humbly with You each day. I come against the lie of control and pride in Jesus name and pray to surrender and humble myself to You. I pray that You will help me when I start to grip too tightly to see Your hand at work and help me to let go. I know Your plans for me are far greater than anything I can think of so I trust You to lead me and to walk with me. Thank you, Lord. In Jesus Name, Amen.

Thoughts

Scripture

"Do nothing out of selfish ambition or vain conceit. Rather, in humility value others above yourselves, not looking to your own interests but each of you to the interests of the others."

-Philippians 2:3-4

Devotional

If you're feeling overwhelmed with all that's on your plate and all you want to accomplish, take a step back today. It's so easy in a busy world to get wrapped up in ourselves even if we don't mean to do it. It's in those moments we have to be aware of any selfish ambition and turn to God for grace to become more selfless. I've found when I focus on serving others and serving God, my problems are no longer top of mind because I know God is taking care of me. I've heard it said that being selfless isn't thinking less of yourself, but thinking of yourself less.

Humility isn't putting yourself down, it's an act of surrender where we admit that God knows best and we loosen the grip we have on our plans. It can also be hard to humble ourselves with the "constant hustle" mentality our culture has today. However, God looks at the heart and He sees everything. While it may seem like those who are looking out for themselves are getting ahead, it's lonely at the top when you are serving yourself. God honors a humble attitude and will promote you in His timing when you do things out of humility.

Prayer

Father, thank you for reminding me what my purpose is through humility. Help me to see and love others how You would. Help me to have more of You and less. Help me to be more selfless and have a servant heart. I come against the lie of the enemy that tells me to be self-focused and help me to focus on Your will for my life. I pray that You would show me ways to serve others through the gifts You've given me. In Jesus name, Amen.

Thoughts

Scripture

"In him we were also chosen, having been predestined according to the plan of him who works out everything in conformity with the purpose of his will, in order that we, who were the first to put our hope in Christ, might be for the praise of his glory."

-Ephesians 1:11-12

Devotional

If you're having trouble letting go and letting God, take comfort in this verse today. It's hard to relinquish control to God when we don't see how things are going to work out. It feels easier to hold tight to what makes sense and what we know. However, God has incredible plans for your life! He designed you and planned for you to be on earth at this very moment in time. He will work everything out as it should be in your life. No matter how far off track we've gotten, God can redeem it. No matter how many pages we have added to our story, He already knows the ending and is working all things together for His glory. God wants to do beautiful and amazing things through your life that will ultimately glorify Him.

Everything in our lives is meant to bring glory to God and give hope to others. Put your hope in Him alone and have faith that He will work out every plan for your life. Remember your identity in Him when life starts to get confusing and chaotic. God also wants to develop our character so that we will be able to live out the dreams He puts on our hearts. Be brave enough to give your plans to God and watch Him make something beautiful out of it all.

Prayer

Father, thank you for the plans You have for me and the purpose You gave me before I was born. Thank you for showing me that when I let go You've got me and have it all under control. I come against the lie of the enemy that tells me I have to do it all myself and I proclaim Your truth that You have my steps ordered. I give You control over all my plans and pray that You'll lead me every step of the way. In Jesus name, Amen.

Thoughts

Scripture

"Consider it pure joy, my brothers and sisters, whenever you face trials of many kinds, because you know that the testing of your faith produces perseverance. Let perseverance finish its work so that you may be mature and complete, not lacking anything."

-James 1:2-4

Devotional

Sometimes life happens and things don't turn out the way we thought it would. It can be hard to find a silver lining when our current situation looks dim. In those moments it can be difficult to seek God. Let this scripture encourage you today. While it may be hard to consider the pain of life as pure joy, choose to look at it from an eternal perspective. In Romans 8:28 scripture tells us that God works all things together for good. When we remember that, we can find joy in knowing God is working everything out for good.

Joy is more than a feeling, it's a fruit of the Spirit. This means it's something we can choose to operate in every day. In our greatest moments of stress, we can choose joy because we have the Holy Spirit in us. We can choose to look at our situation differently and see what we can learn from it. When we face trials, just like a test in school, it grows us. Life's tests grow us spiritually to help us mature if we choose to operate out of the spirit of joy. It's important we take each trial as an opportunity to let go and seek God to grow our faith rather than give into the lie of the enemy that tells us it won't get better. God cares more for you than you realize and the joy comes in knowing he already has the victory. Then we can help others going through the same thing to persevere as well. We all bear fruit whether we realize it or not. We either bear good fruit or bad fruit depending on our reactions. It's up to us.

Prayer

Father, thank you for the joy that we have in You even in the trials of life. Thank you for growing me in my faith so I can continue to grow stronger in my walk with You and share Your hope with others in their trials. I come against the lie of the enemy that tells me it won't get better and I declare Your victory over my situation in Jesus name. I pray You'll show me the things you want me to learn even in these hard moments. In Jesus name, Amen.

Thoughts

Scripture

"Humble yourselves, therefore, under God's mighty hand, that he may lift you up in due time. Cast all your anxiety on him because he cares for you."

-1 Peter 5:6-7

Devotional

Are you feeling worn out and tired in the hustle of life? Do you have dreams that don't seem to be going anywhere? Give it to God today. When we humble ourselves, we are admitting to God that we know He can handle it better than we can and we are trusting Him to carry it for us. We are allowing Him to move in ways only He can by admitting we can't do it all on our own. We aren't designed to do it all on our own. We were designed to do life with God and to bring glory to him through the gifts He's given us. We are meant to partner with God, not take what God gave us and run it on our own. Only He can promote us and lift us up in His timing so that it glorifies Him. When he does, the timing will be perfect and no amount of hustle can change His plan.

If you feel like you've been carrying everything on your own, allow God to step back in today by giving Him control. When we cast our anxiety on Him, he gives us peace by carrying it for us. We have to trust God to help us through our situation. He is preparing us for each step by building our character through each season. He cares deeply for you and wants to walk with you in your situation. The enemy may lie to you by saying God doesn't care, but we see in this scripture that He does care and even wants to take your anxiety for you. When you believe God's truth, the enemy no longer has any power in your life.

Prayer

Father I know You are moving in ways I can't see right now. I'm sorry for carrying my burdens by myself and not giving You control. I trust that You'll work everything out in Your timing. I admit I need to partner with You and allow You to lead me. I come against the lie of the enemy that brings anxiety and I declare Your truth of peace over my life in Jesus name. I give all my worry and anxiety to You today. Thank you for preparing me for each step as You see that I'm ready for it. In Jesus Name, Amen.

Thoughts

Scripture

"In their hearts humans plan their course, but the Lord establishes their steps."

-Proverbs 16:9

Devotional

If you're feeling stressed about your future, pray this verse today. Often times we plan our future down to every little detail and when it doesn't happen in our timing, we get discouraged. God knows better than we do and He hasn't forgotten us. He knows the exact place and time everything in our life should happen. There's so much joy to be found when we do things God's way. I never would have imagined the life for myself that God is unfolding. His plan is so beautiful and He never fails us.

God directs each of our steps and He knows our deepest desires. He'll exceed our wildest dreams for His glory. He also knows our character and wants to prepare our character for our calling. We may think we are ready, but He knows the perfect moment for each step to play out. If He would have allowed me to do the things I'm doing now back when I first had the desire, I wouldn't have been ready. Just like each stage of our life, we have to crawl before we can walk. God cares so much that he wants you to be fully developed for each plan He has for you. I'm so thankful for the way He takes care of us.

Prayer

Father, thank you for the plans and steps You have for me. Thank you for showing me no matter what, You know what You're doing. Teach me to trust You and have faith for what You're doing in the here and now. I come against the lie of the enemy that says I'm forgotten and I declare Your truth that You have established my steps in Jesus name. Give me eyes to see those in my path that You want me to help impact for Your Kingdom. I give You control and humble myself before You, Lord. In Jesus name, Amen.

Thoughts

You are chosen

Ten

Peace, Patience, Waiting

This chapter is for finding peace in the uneasy moments, finding patience when life is difficult and learning to wait on God for His promises. These three things are something I've been learning for several years. It's hard to wait in a world that doesn't share the same standard for boundaries whether it's in a relationship or for a promise. The enemy will lie to us saying we just need to go ahead and make it happen ourselves.

God's truth tells us just how much more incredible life is when we wait on God's timing and the right season. Seasons of waiting can bring on many feelings, but pairing it with patience and peace can make the season bearable when it feels long and hard. God has a plan for you sweet friend and He's moving in ways you might not see, but it's coming! Trust His timing and find encouragement in the scriptures throughout this chapter.

Scripture

"The Lord is not slow in keeping his promise, as some understand slowness. Instead he is patient with you, not wanting anyone to perish, but everyone to come to repentance."

-2 Peter 3:9

Devotional

If you are in a season of waiting today and struggling with trusting God's timing, take heart in this truth. God's timing is perfect. He is preparing you and your promise. He knows every variable and every aspect of the thing you are waiting for in this season. This verse reminds us that God is never slow and He is always on time. Don't give into the lie that He has forgotten you or that your waiting is pointless. Every season matters and God uses every season to teach us something.

Our waiting has purpose and we can still make an impact in our current season. We have to trust that He is forming us for all He is calling us to do. God shows us patience because He doesn't want us to perish. He is more concerned with developing our character first so we can thrive in our calling. He knows our heart and desires. Hold onto this promise today when the waiting gets hard and choose to look at it differently. Choose to see God's hand in preparing you rather than viewing it as Him keeping you from something.

Prayer

Father, thank you for preparing me for my calling. Thank you for Your patience with me so I can thrive in my calling instead of prematurely entering into a season unprepared. I pray for Your timing in the waiting and that You would encourage me with Your truth through the waiting. I come against the lie of the enemy that says You have forgotten me and I declare Your truth, In Jesus name, that You are not slow in keeping Your promise. I trust You, God, and will trust Your timing in my life. In Jesus name, Amen.

Thoughts

Scripture

"For the Lord God is a sun and shield; the Lord bestows favor and honor; no good thing does he withhold from those whose walk is blameless."

-Psalm 84:11

Devotional

If you are struggling with waiting or having patience with God, remember this truth about God's character. God is good and He doesn't withhold anything good from us. He gives us good things and knows exactly what we need and when. He is a shield for us and gives favor and honor. When we follow God and seek His will, He will lead us where we need to go. His desires for you are so much better than your own desires. He purposefully created you and designed you so of course He wants good for you. He knows what will help you and what could hurt you so He protects you. He's always looking out for you.

When a child wants to eat an entire pan of desserts, their parents know what is good for them by only giving them one piece. If the child were to have the entire pan of desserts, they would have a huge stomach ache. Sometimes a child will think their parents are mean for withholding more desserts from them when they are just looking to protect them. Eve was deceived with a similar lie believing God was withholding something good when the Lord was actually protecting her from something harmful. When the enemy tries to feed you the lie that you're missing out or that God is withholding something from you remember this verse. We have to trust that God gives us everything we need at the right time.

Prayer

Father, thank you for Your goodness and protection. Thank you for everything You give me and everything You don't give me. I'm thankful for Your timing. You are so good to me. Give me strength to rest in this truth today. Give me patience through the waiting and help me to see the good things I already have in this season. I come against any lie from the enemy that tells me You are withholding good things from me and I declare the truth that You don't withhold good things from me. In Jesus name, Amen.

Thoughts

Scripture

"But as for me, I watch in hope for the Lord, I wait for God my Savior; my God will hear me."

-Micah 7:7

Devotional

If you are struggling in waiting on God today, remember this truth. God hears you and He is moving on your behalf. His timing is perfect and He will answer your prayer right on time. In the waiting He prepares you and encourages you to have hope. It's often through the impossible and the unseen that God reveals Himself. Often the world causes us to lose hope in the waiting by discouraging us or causing us to doubt what we know God promised. However, God wants us to have hope and faith which often means believing in the unseen or yet to come parts of our story.

Take time to see what He's teaching you in the waiting season and make good use of where He has you right now. Waiting isn't meant to be stagnant, but active. See where He's placed you and use what is in front of you to cultivate this season. You never know what fruit will come if you make good use of where He's put you while you wait. If you do well with what you have you'll bear good fruit for the future. If we don't do anything while we wait, then we won't have as much fruit to bear when the next season comes.

Prayer

Father, thank you for this season of waiting. Help me to continue to have hope in the waiting when the world tells me it's hopeless. Help me to have confidence in Your plans and promises for my life. I pray that You will encourage me through this season and give me patience as I wait for You. I come against any lie that tells me waiting is useless and I declare Your truth in Jesus name that You hear me. Thank you for how You are moving in ways that I can't even see. I trust You, Lord. In Jesus name, amen.

Thoughts

It is Written

"The Lord gives strength to his people; the Lord blesses his people with peace."

-Psalm 29:11

Devotional

If you're feeling a lack of peace today, take heart in this truth about God's strength and peace. He blesses us with His peace. Blessing is an act of favor and adoration from our Father. His peace is of the Spirit, which is deeper than a feeling of peace. The enemy may try to steal our sense of peace by lying to us through fear. By understanding God's love for His people (including you) and God's character in this scripture, we can dismantle the lie of the enemy. If we turn to God, He will bless us with His perfect peace and strengthen us. The Psalms are a great place to turn for whatever you may be feeling because the psalmists experience many of the same feelings as we do in life. God's character, truth and love for us is revealed over and over again through each of the Psalms.

This particular Psalm is written by David. From what we know about David's life, he experienced countless trials and missteps. However, he always recognized where his strength came from and knew that God was his provider. He was able to see God's truth through all his many circumstances. I hope this encourages you today to find peace through God and rely on him for your strength. Look in the Psalms for God's character and what God's says about His people to continually have this truth in your heart.

Prayer

Father, thank you for the peace that only You can provide. I know my strength and peace come from You alone. Please help me in my current situation to have peace and strengthen my faith. I pray You'll help me through what I'm currently dealing with. I come against the lie of the enemy that brings fear and I declare Your Peace in my life in Jesus name. Holy Spirit, please provide an overwhelming sense of peace today. In Jesus Name, Amen.

Thoughts

Scripture

"But the fruit of the spirit is love, joy, peace, forbearance, kindness, goodness, faithfulness, gentleness and self-control. Against such there is no law."

-Galatians 5:22-23

Devotional

The fruit of the Spirit is always a great truth to hold onto no matter what you're feeling. God is love and He bears these fruits. Whatever you are feeling today weigh it against the fruit of the Spirit and God's love. If you are feeling uneasy and don't have peace, take time to identify the cause and pray against it. Ask God for the fruit of the Spirit, especially peace.

Part of understanding God's truth is taking our thoughts captive. Our thoughts have the power to rule our lives. It's the very reason there are so many scriptures regarding our thoughts. Our minds are a powerful place, but they are no match for God's truth and His power. We have free will, but when we surrender and seek God He can provide us these fruits that will make our lives so much better.

Our feelings have a tendency to take the wheel from time to time. This comes when our alignment is off and we allow our soul to drive. We have to realign Spirit, soul, then body. It's time we let the Spirit become the driver again. Someone once told me that our feelings can ride in the car with us, we just can't allow them to be in the driver's seat. We need to realize that for every fruit of the Spirit, the enemy has an opposite to use against us. When we should have peace, the enemy attacks with fear. When we should have joy, the enemy attacks with depression. We can have peace if we will declare it through God to cast aside the dis-ease we feel. We have power through the Holy Spirit and Jesus name.

Prayer

Father, thank you for this truth today. Please help me weigh my thoughts and feelings against the fruit of the Spirit. Help me to produce the fruit of the Spirit in my life. I pray for peace today and ask that You will help me take every thought captive that may affect that feeling. I ask for your protection. I come against any lie of the enemy and declare Your truth in my life. In Jesus name, Amen.

Thoughts

Scripture

"May God himself, the God of peace, sanctify you through and through. May your whole spirit, soul and body be kept blameless at the coming of our Lord Jesus Christ. The one who calls you is faithful, and he will do it."

-1 Thessalonians 5:23-24

Devotional

If you're feeling restless today and can't seem to find peace remember we serve the God of peace. When the enemy tries to deceive you into believing you can't achieve peace, declare this truth. God wants to sanctify you (set you apart) so you may fully know Him. He desires a close, personal relationship with you. He is faithful and He will provide. I love this verse because it clearly reminds us of God's character. Often times when we begin to allow doubt to fill our minds, it's because we began to doubt God's character. When we hold onto the truth of who God is, we are reminded of who we are.

When we keep our eyes on Him and draw close to Him, we will continually find His peace. It's easy to let the world bring chaos into our lives that distract us from God. It's a daily discipline to seek after God's character. That's why this verse calls out our whole spirit, soul and body must be kept blameless. That's our entire being… our emotions, our fleshly desires and spiritual desires. It's also listed in the order it is on purpose. Our spirit should be what leads us with our soul (feelings) next and lastly our body (fleshly desires). When we do things in the right order we will have peace and the ability to trust God in the midst of chaos.

Prayer

Father, thank you for this truth today. I pray You will help me to have Your peace each day. Sanctify me, Lord. Help my spirit, soul and body to align with You and my spirit to lead. Help me to find peace even in the chaos. Help me to keep my eyes on you and not on my circumstances. Show me each day Your character and remind me of who You created me to be. In Jesus Name, Amen.

Thoughts

Scripture

"For the revelation awaits an appointed time; it speaks of the end and will not prove false. Though it linger, wait for it; it will certainly come and will not delay."

-Habakkuk 2:3

Devotional

If you're struggling with a season of waiting, let this truth encourage you. God has an appointed time for everything in our lives. It all plays into a larger plan and we get to be a part of that plan. God always comes through on His promises. He's not delaying, but orchestrating the perfect timing. During moments of waiting, we have to keep our focus on God and eternity. It's easy to get focused on our circumstances and to only see what's right in front of us. We begin to only think of our part in the story rather than the larger part of the story God is writing. There are so many pieces in play that go into making your story weave into God's grander story.

If we can focus on all God is doing while we wait for our answered prayer, it will be a little easier to wait. While it may seem like the waiting season is lingering, keep waiting and keep trusting. When God comes through He doesn't do anything half way. He hasn't forgotten about you. Take this time while waiting to grow in trusting and leaning on God. Take this time to focus on the present and see how He can use you in this moment. I've been through many waiting seasons and I know how tough it can be. God knows as well and He only has your best interest in mind in what He's preparing for you.

Prayer

Father, Thank you for this truth today about seasons of waiting. Help me focus on You and learn to continually trust you. I know trusting and leaning on You is a daily choice so help me to stay close to You. I pray against doubt, fear and anxiousness that comes with waiting and replace it with Your truth and Your goodness. In Jesus name, Amen.

Thoughts

Acknowledgments

To all my friends who offered encouragement, support and assistance on this dream project. I'm beyond grateful for the friendship I have with each of you and thankful for your continued support.

To my mom, You have been my constant cheerleader and always supportive of my desire to chase my dreams. Thank you for raising me to be a strong woman and to love Jesus.

To my family, thank you for always encouraging me and for being supportive of all my endeavors.

To Stacey, thank you for your help in editing this book and for constantly encouraging me not to give up.

To my church, thank you for being a community that encourages us to find our God-given dreams and live out our purpose.

To Antoinette, thank you for being a constant encourager in my life and for being a godly mentor. Thank you for pushing me to constantly grow and chase my dreams.

To God and my Savior, Jesus, thank you for allowing me to steward this dream and for allowing me to be the vessel for this message. I'm so thankful that you chose me and I pray you will touch so many lives through this book. Thank you for never giving up on me.

About the Author

Courtney Hope Wilson is a millennial writer with a passion for leading leaders, developing dreams in this generation and helping others live out their God-given purpose. She is the founder of The Trailblazer Journals, an online community dedicated to developing God-dreams. She is also the founder of the Little Creative Company, a small design agency dedicated to helping non-profits, Christian organizations, churches and dreamers develop their brand, websites and dreams.

Connect with us:
courtneyhopewilson.com
@courthopewilson

thetrailblazerjournals.com
@thetrailblazerjournals.

littlecreativecompany.com
@littlecreativecompany

The Trailblazer Journals is an online community where we believe our generation is called to be trailblazers. Our goal is to encourage people to find their God-given purpose, live out their dreams, build their leadership skills and blaze the trail for God's kingdom. We are real people who are poised for purpose.

Connect with us at thetrailblazerjournals.com and @thetrailblazerjournals on social media.

Little Creative Company is a small design agency dedicated to helping non-profits, Christian organizations, churches and dreamers develop their brand, website and turn their dream into a reality. Little Creative Press is an imprint of Little Creative Company.

Connect with us at littlecreativecompany.com or @littlecreativecompany on Instagram.